T0339518

# Cambridge Elements ≡

Elements in Leadership
edited by
Ronald Riggio
*Claremont McKenna College*
Susan Murphy
*University of Edinburgh*
Founding Editor
Georgia Sorenson
*University of Cambridge*

# LEADING FOR INNOVATION

*Leadership Actions to Enhance Follower Creativity*

Michael D Mumford
*The University of Oklahoma*

Tanner R Newbold
*The University of Oklahoma*

Mark Fichtel
*The University of Oklahoma*

Samantha England
*The University of Oklahoma*

CAMBRIDGE
UNIVERSITY PRESS

# CAMBRIDGE
## UNIVERSITY PRESS

University Printing House, Cambridge CB2 8BS, United Kingdom

One Liberty Plaza, 20th Floor, New York, NY 10006, USA

477 Williamstown Road, Port Melbourne, VIC 3207, Australia

314–321, 3rd Floor, Plot 3, Splendor Forum, Jasola District Centre, New Delhi – 110025, India

103 Penang Road, #05–06/07, Visioncrest Commercial, Singapore 238467

Cambridge University Press is part of the University of Cambridge.

It furthers the University's mission by disseminating knowledge in the pursuit of education, learning, and research at the highest international levels of excellence.

www.cambridge.org
Information on this title: www.cambridge.org/9781108811705
DOI: 10.1017/9781108867887

© Michael D Mumford 2022
*The University of Oklahoma*
Tanner R Newbold
*The University of Oklahoma*
Mark Fichtel
*The University of Oklahoma*
Samantha England
*The University of Oklahoma*

First published 2022

*A catalogue record for this publication is available from the British Library.*

ISBN 978-1-108-81170-5 Paperback
ISSN 2631-7796 (online)
ISSN 2631-7788 (print)

# Leading for Innovation

## Leadership Actions to Enhance Follower Creativity

Elements in Leadership

DOI: 10.1017/9781108867887
First published online: May 2022

Michael D Mumford
*The University of Oklahoma*
Tanner R Newbold
*The University of Oklahoma*
Mark Fichtel
*The University of Oklahoma*
Samantha England
*The University of Oklahoma*

**Author for correspondence:** Michael D Mumford, mmumford@ou.edu

**Abstract:** Creativity, the generation of novel and useful ideas, and innovation, the transformation of these ideas into new products, processes, and services, are both critical for the long-term viability, profitability, and growth of organizations. Moreover, the complex, risky, and uncertain nature of innovative efforts demonstrates the importance of organizational leaders to effectively manage the innovative process. In this Element, we discuss the role of leaders in effectively facilitating the creative problem-solving process that gives rise to innovative products, processes, and services. More specifically, we highlight the knowledge, skills, and behaviors needed to effectively lead across three integrated facets of this process: leading the people, leading the work, and leading the firm. This discussion promotes an understanding of how leaders manage those asked to engage in innovative efforts and, moreover, how leaders systematically integrate creative ideas within the organization to ensure the development and success of innovative products, processes, or services.

**Keywords:** leadership, innovation, creativity, management, problem-solving

ISBNs: 9781108811705 (PB), 9781108867887 (OC)
ISSNs: 2631-7796 (online), 2631-7788 (print)

# Contents

# 1 Creativity and Innovation in Organizations

There is little doubt our lives, and progress in our world ultimately, are driven by innovation. When we think of the new inventions, new discoveries, new processes, new music, new forms of entertainment that so enrich our lives, however, we typically think in romantic terms. We ascribe the innovation we find so appealing to the genius of a single individual. We see the innovation as an outcome of a mysterious, almost magical, process using terms such as insight, incubation, and imagination to describe how these innovations are born into the world. The innovator, a single person, is seen as a hero battling the social forces, people, competitors, and government, which hope to destroy the magic that brought this innovation to life. As much as we may love this image of innovation, it is garbage.

Consider just a few examples. We consider Walt Disney a great creator. Gabler (2007) describes a career where his success, and the firm's success, was based on the progressive exploitation of new technologies, recruitment of talented artists, and careful sourcing and editing of material. Another example may be found in Steve Jobs – an innovative hero in the world of technology. As Isaacson (2011) reminds us, however, the innovations that flowed from Apple were as much, if not more so, due to the work of a talented cadre of engineers as Jobs' careful imposition of design and usability constraints on the work of those engineers. We assume that firms working in high technology arose from the genius and vision of eminent engineers such as Andy Grove of Intel. As Gertner (2012) reminds us, however, the success of Intel is as much attributable to earlier work done at Bell Labs and the support of the United States government as the "genius" of Andy Grove.

These few examples serve to make our basic point that much of what we assume about innovation is quite simply wrong. The reality of innovation is far less romantic than we commonly assume. It is far more prosaic, and it is from institutions, both government and industrial organizations, that innovations emerge. And, because innovations emerge from institutions, academic, governmental, industrial, and nonprofit, it is not at all unreasonable to assume that leadership will prove critical to the development and adoption of virtually all innovations (Mumford & Licuanan, 2004). In this Element, we will examine what those asked to lead innovative efforts must do. Before turning to the leadership of innovative efforts, however, it would seem germane to understand why innovation is important to institutions.

## 1.1 What Is a Firm?

Katz and Kahn (1978) provide what is perhaps the most succinct description of exactly what we mean by the term firm or institution. Firms are ultimately based on a division of labor, with the division of labor resulting in both greater expertise on the part of workers and greater efficiency in the production of goods and services sought by stakeholders – often, but not always, a firm's customers. A firm uses this division of labor to produce goods and services of value to stakeholders who, in turn, provide resources to the firm for access to those goods and services.

A firm must organize itself in such a way as to transform inputs, materials, and information into these valued goods and services. Thus, firms, or institutions, structure the work done by people in this division of labor to produce goods and services as efficiently as possible. Accordingly, in describing firms, we will speak of key functional units: manufacturing, purchasing, sales, and so on. The nature of, and relationships among, these functional units is what we mean when we speak of the "firm."

The activities that occur in these functional units, of course, must be organized, evaluated, and directed (Bass & Bass, 2008). It is the role of the leaders in a firm to organize, evaluate, and direct the activities of functional units and the people who work in these units in such a way as to maximize the resources returned to the firm and optimize the efficiency of the firm's transformation process (Yukl, 2011).

Firms seek to maintain and enhance the efficiency, and value, of the products and services they produce. Often we assume firms simply seek stability through control of markets, supplies, and the transformation process. Firms, however, exist in a competitive world where change occurs over time. This rather straightforward observation has many notable implications. First, firm activities must be directed as much to the future as to the present to allow adaptation to change (Jacobs & Jaques, 1991). Second, firms must explore their environment, and their future, as well as exploit their current efficiency in the transformation process (March, 1991). Third, firms must learn about the opportunities that might arise in the future to be able to exploit emergent affordances in such a way as to enhance the value of their products and processes (Kogut & Zander, 1996). Put more succinctly, firms are not rigid, fixed entities but instead are best conceived of as adaptive, evolving, learning entities as they seek to both explore and exploit a dynamic, and potentially chaotic, environment.

## 1.2 Why Is Innovation of Value?

Traditionally, it was thought firms simply sought stability – stability that inherently rules out the value of innovation. Adaptation to a chaotic, changing environment, however, requires innovation. And, in fact, innovation is a key to the founding, success, and survival of firms. The founding of a new firm, an entrepreneurial activity, is typically based on innovations in technology, process, and markets (Schumpeter, 2000; Wong, Ho, & Autio, 2005). These new firms may seek to exploit an emergent technology, often a technology "stolen" or borrowed from others with further development, but not always. Sometimes innovation in productive processes or markets can allow new firms to develop and thrive. Regardless of the basis on which a new firm is established, innovation is a key requirement.

Once established, firms select, or create, a strategy they believe will support and sustain their operations over time. Miles and Snow (1978) describe four types of strategies seen in firms: prospectors, analyzers, defenders, and reactors. Defender firms generally discount the need for innovation, seeking to maximize returns from an extent system. Reactors will innovate when necessary. Firms settling on a prospector (e.g., 3M) or analyzer (e.g., IBM) strategy, however, see innovation as critical to the fundamental existence of the firm. Thus, their business and business strategy is inherently bound to ongoing chains of innovation – typically with respect to certain fundamentals such as long-chain polymers in the case of Du Pont. And, in prospector and analyzer firms, firm success is explicitly tied to the development and deployment of innovations. Thus, a firm's founding, and often its strategic approach to the "business," is inherently tied to innovation.

Perhaps more importantly, firm success appears tied to innovation. One key index of the success of a firm is its survival. Firms come and go but our best firms remain with us over time. Cefis and Marsili (2005) examined survival, or time in business, among Dutch manufacturing firms. They found that firm innovations, both technological and process innovations, extend firm life expectancy irrespective of firm age, size, or markets. Indeed, Naidoo (2010) found that firms' ability to weather, or survive, external crises, such as economic downturns, often depends on the timely development and deployment of innovative products and services. Thus, innovations can represent a kind of firm insurance policy. Regardless, however, a firm's long-term survival seems to depend on its capacity for innovation.

Innovation, however, is not just critical to firm survival. The profits and growth of firms also seem to be tied to innovation. For example, Scherer (1965) showed that firm patent rates, one marker of innovation focused on technical innovation, were strongly related to firm profitability and growth in size with the value of those innovations far outweighing the costs entailed in their development. Howitt and Aghion (1998) reach the same conclusion, noting that firm innovation in technology results in growth of profits that outweigh investment costs. Indeed, it is not only innovations in technology that contribute to increased profits and growth – innovations in marketing, purchasing, logistics, and human resources have similar effects (Berger et al., 2009).

Not only is innovation critical to the founding, strategy, profitability, and survival of firms, it has a number of less tangible, but nonetheless valuable, benefits for firms. The employees of innovative firms are happier and more committed to their organizations. It is easier for innovative firms to recruit talented workers. Customers are more committed to firms fielding innovative products. And, innovative firms are more likely to be responsible citizens investing more in their communities – both the business community and local communities.

## 1.3 Why Is Innovation Hard?

Given the impact of firm innovation on profit, growth, and survival, one would expect firms to innovate all the time. Firms *may* want innovation but, in point of fact, innovation in firms is relatively rare. Many attributes of firms militate against innovation. To begin, development and deployment of an innovation is costly – often substantially so. For example, drug companies may spend hundreds of millions of dollars to develop a new treatment, and, even if viable, it may not sell well enough to justify such an enormous expenditure. Thus, it may not always be in the firm's best interest to pursue an innovation. To complicate matters further, even a viable innovation may not "fit" with the firm's extant processes or extant markets. As a result, the firm may not have the capabilities needed to successfully exploit an innovation (Osborn & Marion, 2009).

It is not only the costs associated with development of an innovation that are of concern. Firm efficiencies depend on a stable, or reasonably stable, process for transforming inputs into viable products. And, any innovation to some extent will disrupt the efficiency of this transformation process. The cost of innovation to efficiency is one reason why many firms look at innovation as a risk. What should be recognized here, moreover, are the norms and work processes of those in a firm are tied to, and to an extent embedded in, extant work activities – activities likely to be disrupted by innovation. To make matters even worse, people may, and often do, see innovations as a threat to their skills, expertise, and employability. And, loss of skill, the entailed loss of value, and the potential violation of norms and extant business processes all will lead people to react negatively, strongly negatively, to innovative efforts (Blair & Mumford, 2007).

The cost and social disruption attached to innovation, however, are not the only forces that will lead firms to reject innovative efforts. One issue here is technical. Innovation comes, technically, when there is a readiness for the innovation (Wise, 1992). And, often a field is simply not ready to develop even the most promising technologies. Another issue arises because innovative efforts, despite even substantial investments, often fail (Huber, 1998). Firms do not like to spend resources on failures, and people in firms do not like to fail. Still another reason why firms reject innovative efforts is the nature of the innovation that may undermine, or kill, existing product lines (Chandy & Tellis, 1998). Innovations, moreover, may prove too easy for other firms to imitate or may have to short a cycle of ownership by the firm – both forces that act to undermine the value of innovation (Bessen & Maskin, 2009).

To complicate matters even further, it is clear that successful firms must "stick to the knitting" building expertise and business processes with respect to certain key fundamentals applying in a certain business area (Hounshell, 1992). Innovations incongruent, or inconsistent, with these fundamentals cannot be readily understood, or efficiently exploited, by a firm (Licuanan, Dailey, & Mumford, 2007). Simply not understanding an idea, or its implications, makes it difficult for firms to adapt, or support, innovative efforts.

## 1.4 Where Does It Occur?

Clearly, firms experience real pressures to innovate; yet, at the same time, they confront real pressures not to innovate. This quandary, however, poses a question. Where and when are firms willing to adopt innovative ideas? We will start here by examining the environment in which firms operate and its impact on innovation. Ford, Sharfman, and Dean (2008) examined firms' willingness to take creative/innovative strategic decisions with respect to environmental influences. They found that firms made innovative decisions when the environment in which the firm was operating was technically complex and turbulent. Competitive pressure and resource availability, ease of obtaining finance on high rates, also have been found to contribute to firms' willingness to innovate. Firm capital intensity, or infrastructure requirements, however, militates against innovation. Thus, firms seem especially willing to innovate in complex turbulent environments where resources are available to support the costs of an innovative effort.

Damanpour and Aravind (2012) have examined how the structural characteristics of firms contribute to their innovations. In this meta-analytic study, two key characteristics of firms were identified that contributed to innovation. First, the firms were relatively flat, implying that innovation was not inhibited by multiple layers of critical evaluations. Second, these firms were typically professionalized – implying that technical, professional, evaluation structures, and a focus on professional contributions are critical for innovation. Notably, however, neither firm size nor the level of bureaucracy in the firm inhibited innovation. In fact, size and bureaucracy were positively related to innovation. Although these findings might at first glance seem counterintuitive, one must remember size provides resources and bureaucracy serves to *minimize* the "off-task" burden placed on those doing creative work.

The influence of firm professionalization on innovation, moreover, points to another characteristic of firms contributing to innovation. Innovative firms focus on a limited set of fundamentals relevant to the firm and the profession. Thus, Hounshell (1992) describes Du Pont's focus on organic chemistry, while Gertner (2012) describes AT&T's focus on communications. This focus on professional fundamentals, however, is noteworthy for another reason. Innovative firms value learning with respect to those fundamentals (Silverberg & Verspagen, 1994). Indeed, innovative firms not only establish, and value, structures supporting learning (Calantone, Cavusgil, & Zhao, 2002), learning is considered of sufficient value that the value of learning will offset the cost associated with failed innovative efforts (Mumford & Hunter, 2005).

In firms working in a turbulent, resource-rich, professionalized environment, where learning is valued with respect to fundamentals, one might expect to see innovation. In this regard, however, it is important to recognize that there is not one form of innovation one might see in such firms. Accordingly, it is common to speak of product and process innovations (Boer & During, 2001). Although we often assume product innovations are hard, difficult to execute, in firms, process innovations, changes in human resources recruiting, for example, may be as difficult, if not more difficult, to develop and field due to institutional resistance. Perhaps, more significantly, product and process innovations must often be tied together in an integrated system of innovations. A case in point may be found in Ford's work on automotive assembly lines (Wilson, 2014).

Some of these innovative efforts may be professionally significant and others less so (McKay & Kaufman, 2020). What is of note here, however, is that chains of innovation are typically required to produce viable new products, and the success of the product will depend on the various pieces of these chains working in harmony. A case in point may be found in shipping containers, a viable technical innovation, but one which also requires new cranes, new docks, and new truck designs. Thus, innovation in a firm may require new production procedures, new staff, and the establishment of new markets.

One implication of our foregoing observations is that cross-functional teams are often required as an innovative product, or process, moves from initial development to fielding (Mumford, Bedell-Avers, & Hunter, 2008). The need for input from other functional units, such as manufacturing and marketing, may well prove crucial to the success of an innovative effort. In this regard, however, it is important to bear in mind that bringing in new people and new functional perspectives may have some noteworthy disruptive effects for the team working on an innovation. To complicate matters even further, innovative experts may need to be placed in other areas, for example manufacturing in the case of technical innovation, to help those units cope with the implications of an innovation in further day-to-day operations (Mumford, Bedell-Avers, & Hunter, 2008). These observations are noteworthy because they imply that there are a lot of moving parts, and a lot of moving people, in any innovative effort.

The complex nature of an innovative effort, moving people, additions and subtractions of expertise, and chains of product, process, marketing, and financial innovations, implies one cannot be certain about the ultimate outcome of any innovative effort. It may work, then again, it may not. And, whether an innovation works or not may be a result of multiple considerations: Was the product, or idea, bad, were we lacking a needed innovation in production, did we miss something that made the product difficult to use? One implication of this observation is that innovation in firms is not simply a matter of coming up with an idea or prototype. Instead, the innovative effort must be managed as an unfolding, dynamic program as ideas are developed and progressively reconfigured. One implication of this observation is that a series of decisions must be made as to whether a program will continue and how it will continue with the cost and complexity of the program increasing as an initial idea proceeds to fielding. Moreover, different criteria must be applied at different stages as ideas move to fielding – for example, scanning efforts, initial exploratory efforts, should be appraised in terms of learning potential, prototypes should be appraised in terms of deployment feasibility, and initial products should be appraised in terms of market potential (Mumford, Bedell-Avers, & Hunter, 2008). Thus, different standards must be applied at different points in managing an innovative effort.

A complex program of work involving chains of big, and small, innovations is noteworthy for another reason. In complex efforts we cannot with assurance say exactly how things will turn out. Thus, innovative efforts require ongoing program management, hands-on program management, where progress and pitfalls are constantly reviewed. Accordingly, innovative firms are characterized by meetings, both informal meeting among those vested in a certain part of the work and formal meetings where progress to date and problems encountered are explicitly addressed. Put differently, innovative efforts are characterized by the weekly review meeting and intense, active communication among those involved in the innovative effort (Perry, 1993).

Of course, complex systems of enterprise require active, ongoing monitoring and feedback. Indeed, innovative firms seek to create and value feedback concerning the work being executed – often monitoring feedback from multiple sources, including the profession, competitors, customers, and regulators. In complex programs, however, feedback is not always positive. Crises do occur, a point made in a qualitative study by Drazin, Glynn, and Kazanjian (1999). They observed the process, and meetings, surrounding the development of a new aircraft. They found that crises not only routinely emerged but that some crises clearly were also threats to the success of the project. Focused, intense, action was often required to address these emergent crises – crises that sometimes could only be resolved through creative thinking and a new chain of innovative work.

These observations are noteworthy with respect to the people actually doing the creative work. Our stereotypic image of the creative person is a relaxed person freely exploring the implications of their unique ideas. No one behaves this way when they are confronting a crisis. Instead, what one sees is an intense focus and a persistent drive to resolve the problem at hand. Indeed, Furnham (2020) has found that obsession and persistence are two characteristics one most commonly sees in those working on innovative projects. This obsessive persistence, however, is also accompanied by substantial expertise (Ericsson & Charness, 1999), a desire for autonomy (Liu, Chen, & Yao, 2011), and a critical, often self-critical, approach to the work (Gibson & Mumford, 2013). The problem here, of course, is critical; autonomous experts obsessed with their *own* technical problem and persistently trying to resolve this problem are not the most tractable workforce – a workforce likely to see a crisis in different ways, appraise feedback from a unique perspective, and likely to be unwilling to stick to the plan, either the project plan or the plans formulated for addressing a project crisis.

## 1.5 Why Leadership?

Our foregoing observations are noteworthy because they point to why leadership is so crucial to successful innovation. On the one hand, firms need innovation to grow, profit, and survive. However, innovation is needed, and valued, in a complex, technically turbulent environment. In complex, technically turbulent operating environments, especially when competition is intense and competitors are taking their own approach to a problem, it is unclear how the firm should proceed in its attempts to innovate. And, this lack of clarity calls for effective leadership of innovative efforts.

With respect to the firm, however, leaders cannot assume full, uncompromising support. Innovative efforts are costly, and the risk of failure is high.

Appraisals of cost and risk may result in even the most promising ideas being dropped. Not only will objective evaluations of cost and risk act to undermine innovative efforts, the nature of the firm, its embedded processes, peoples' investments in the correct way of doing things, and the lack of a clear path to an assured product, all may act to lead firms to reject innovative efforts even though risk and costs seem objectively low. Under these conditions, innovative projects are likely to move forward only when they have champions – champions who are leaders with respect to the innovative effort (Markham & Smith, 2017).

These champions, leaders of innovative efforts, however, are presented with a task of unusual complexity. Not only must they assure the willingness of the firm to support the innovative effort, they must also manage a program of work – a program that will involve not only multiple technical innovations but also multiple process innovations – some big and some small. And, in this program requisite innovations must be structured into an integrated chain of innovations where the weakest link may act to undermine an otherwise promising venture.

As the leader seeks to develop and manage a chain of innovations, a complex set of interactions will act to condition the success of innovative efforts. Leaders must reach out to other vested interests in the firm. Leaders must help others grapple with the implications of an innovation. Leaders must encourage viable collaborations and ongoing cross talk, both within and outside the firm, to build strong innovations. The work arising from these collaborations must be appropriately evaluated. And, crises arising from the work must be addressed. Put differently, the work, sometimes technical, sometimes, social we are asking the leaders of innovative efforts to do is truly daunting.

To make matters even more complex, the people they are asked to lead are themselves uniquely demanding. They are critical, autonomous, obsessive, and persistent. This is not a group of people who can be guaranteed to go along with a plan, and they may not be a group who will get along with each other especially well. Somehow, the leader must get the best out of these people, channeling their critical, obsessive persistence into the innovative effort at hand – an effort that may or may not work out.

Our foregoing observations, in fact, lay out the key goals we will cover in this Element. First, we will examine how those asked to lead innovative efforts should lead the work. Second, we will examine how those asked to lead innovative efforts should lead the people doing the work. Third, we will examine how those asked to lead innovative efforts should lead the firm in its search for viable innovations. Before turning to leading the work, the team, and the firm, we will examine what we know about the nature of creative work and the type of people who are willing to undertake the creative work that provides the basis for innovation in firms.

## 2 Creativity and Creative People

Although firms see the risk in pursuing innovations, profitability, growth, and survival all act to encourage innovation in many forms. What should be recognized here, however, is that innovations do not arise in a vacuum. Innovations ultimately come from people's creative thinking. Thus, to ensure innovation, firms must encourage creative thinking by at least some of the firm's workers. Understanding creative thinking, and the contextual conditions, or the environment, which encourages creative thought, provides the foundation for any effort intended to encourage innovation (Mumford & Hunter, 2005). More centrally, leaders, in a search for innovation, must manage workers in such a way as to encourage creative thinking. Accordingly, in this section, we will consider what we know about creative thinking (cognition), the nature of creative people (personality), and what leads people to invest in creative work (motivation).

### 2.1 What Is Creativity?

When one uses the word creativity, images, stereotype images, are called to mind of the crazy artist, Lady Gaga, or the disheveled scientist, Albert Einstein. Certainly, works in the arts and sciences often require creativity (Feist & Gorman, 1998). When seeking to understand exactly what is meant by the term creativity, however, it is best to put these stereotypes aside (Mumford, 2000).

Initial definitions of creativity were externally referenced. Thus, creativity was held to be reflected in accomplishments, real-world accomplishments, deemed by others to be creative, such as Nobel Prizes, Oscars, or patent awards (Simonton, 1984). Of course, awards of this sort depend on others' evaluations of the work accomplishments (McClelland, 1961). Thus, the question arises as to exactly what underlies others' appraisals of work as creative.

Some initial answers to this question have been provided in studies by Besemer and O'Quin (1998) and Christiaans (2002). In these studies, expert judges were presented with an array of creative products – for example, furniture designs. They were asked to rate these products on a variety of attributes, and these attribute ratings were factored to identify the dimensions reflecting key attributes of creative products. Three dimensions consistently emerged: quality, originality, and elegance. The products reflecting these attributes are what is meant by the term creative.

Here, however, one must ask another question: What is the nature of the tasks that allow people to produce high-quality, original, and elegant products? An initial answer to this question was provided by Guilford (1950), who argued that the production of high-quality, original, and elegant products required people to generate multiple alternative ideas – potential problem solutions. This observation was the basis for work in divergent thinking. This observation, however, leaves unanswered a fundamental question: producing lots of ideas to what? Mumford and Gustafson (2007), however, provided an answer to this question, arguing that it is production of ideas for solving a certain type of problem that provides the basis for creative accomplishment. Specifically, they argued that creativity is based on the production of high-quality, original, and elegant solutions to novel, complex, and ill-defined, or poorly structured, problems.

This definition of what is meant by the term creativity is noteworthy for many reasons. First, sometimes a single high-quality, original, and elegant problem solution may lead others to appraise someone's work as creative (Reiter-Palmon, 2018). Second, creativity comes in many forms depending on the nature of the problem, Bic "C" creativity or small "c" creativity and the nature of the person – a novel, complex, ill-defined problem to one person may not be a novel, complex, ill-defined problem to another (McKay & Kaufman, 2020). Third, creativity is ultimately a form of high-level cognition, or thinking, where the person has discretion as to exactly how much effort they will in invest in problem-solving.

## 2.2 How Do People Solve Creative Problems?

So what are the cognitive operations, processes, people must perform to produce creative problem solutions? This question has intrigued scholars for more than 100 years, and many models of creative thinking processes having been proposed (Dewey, 1910; Parnes & Noller, 1972; Sternberg, 1988; Wallas, 1926). Mumford et al. (1991) conducted a review of the various models of creative processing activities, or thinking activities, that have been proposed over the years. They identified eight core, critical processing activities involved in most incidents of creative performance. These processes were used to formulate the model presented in Figure 1. More specifically, these eight core processes were held to include (1) problem definition, (2) information gathering, (3) concept/case selection, (4) conceptual combination, (5) idea generation, (6) idea evaluation, (7) implementation planning, and (8) adaptive monitoring.

Evidence for the validity of this process model has been obtained in an extensive series of studies by Mumford and his colleagues (e.g., Baughman & Mumford, 1995; Lonergan, Scott, & Mumford, 2004; Mumford et al., 1997;

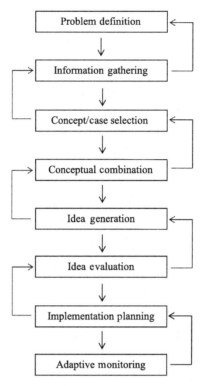

**Figure 1** Process model of creative problem-solving

Osburn & Mumford, 2006). Broadly speaking, in each study a task was devised to isolate a single process. For example, in information gathering, how long people spent reading cards presenting different types of information bearing on a problem, or in conceptual combination, combine bat, glove, net (sport equipment) with robin, ostrich, owl (birds). The effectiveness with which people executed each process was assessed and used to account for performance, as appraised by judges' evaluations of quality, originality, and elegance of solutions to creative problems drawn from the marketing, educational, public policy, and military domains. It was found that the effective execution of each process was strongly positively ($r \cong .35$) related to the production of creative problem solutions. Effective execution of multiple processes was very strongly related ($R \cong .60$), given reliabilities in the .80's, to the quality originality, and elegance of problem solutions. Each process made a unique, incremental contribution to predicting creative problem-solving, and it predicted performance better than other characteristics of the person (e.g., personality, divergent thinking). Moreover, errors flowed through process execution. Friedrich and Mumford (2009) found that errors in problem definition disrupted information gathering.

Because errors flow through processes, creative problem-solving is a risky venture where success is not assured.

Within this model, each process is held to involve multiple operations – some operations being convergent and others being divergent. Thus, in conceptual combination, to produce viable new ways of understanding problems, people must (1) identify shared and nonshared features of concepts, (2) map shared and nonshared features, (3) use common elements to allow new features to emerge, and (4) elaborate extensively on emergent new features (Scott, Lonergan, & Mumford, 2005). In idea evaluation, people must (1) define appraisal standards, (2) appraise ideas to meeting evaluation standards, (3) forecast the downstream strengths and weaknesses of ideas, and (4) compensate for idea deficiencies (Lonergan, Scott, & Mumford, 2004). Thus, execution of each process is a complex, highly demanding activity where the products of process execution must be appraised. With regard to the operations involved in executing each of these creative thinking processes, assumptions we often make about how to manage people's work do not seem to apply. For example, in defining problems, people should think about procedures and constraints, not goals. In gathering information, it is not enough to just gather key facts; they must also think about anomalies implied by these facts. In concept/case selection, concepts, flexible concepts pointing to causes, errors, and applications are to be retrieved. In conceptual combination, extensive, time-consuming elaboration on emergent new features is required. In idea generation, generation to application, not open unconstrained generation, is required. In idea evaluation, it is not enough to evaluate; people must try to improve idea deficiencies. In implementation planning, people must identify and find ways to work around key constraints. In adaptive monitoring, people must identify and constantly monitor key diagnostics – acting to exploit emergent opportunities. Execution of all these processing operations improves as people practice and acquire procedural knowledge for working in a domain.

Our foregoing observations, however, point to the importance of expertise in creative problem-solving. Indeed, most prior work indicates that those who provide creative problem solutions have substantial expertise working in the domain at hand (Ericsson & Charness, 1994). For example, Clydesdale (2006) found that substantial practice, deliberate practice, allowing people to evaluate and seek to improve their performance, was critical to the creative achievements of the Beatles. Connelly et al. (2000) assessed the expertise of Army leaders based on a task sort where sorting tasks into categories consistent with Army leadership models was used to appraise expertise. Some 1800 Army officers were also asked to solve creative problems where a modified think aloud protocol was used to assess the effectiveness of process execution. It was found that greater expertise was related to more effective execution of all the creative thinking process, with process execution being positively related to both critical incident performance and medals won.

Clearly, knowledge and expertise are critical to execution of creative thinking processes – creative people are experts. However, one might also ask exactly what type of knowledge experts use when solving creative problems? This issue has been addressed in a study by Hunter et al. (2008). In this study, a training manipulation was used to prime, or encourage, people to apply conceptual (i.e., schematic) knowledge, case-based (i.e., experiential) knowledge, or associational (i.e., connections) knowledge prior to working on a social innovation problem where judges appraised the quality, originality, and elegance of problem solutions. They found that creative problem solutions emerged from the use of concepts, cases, or a combination of both. Thus, creative people need both "book" knowledge and "bench" skills, or real-world experience. In yet another study, Scott, Lonergan, and Mumford (2005) asked people to work with either concepts or cases in solving a creative educational leadership problem. They found that the highest quality and most original solutions emerged when people employed many concepts but just a few critical prototypic cases due to the complexity of the case-based knowledge – cases include information about causes, actions, restrictions, resources, actors, and outcomes. Although this finding is not surprising, it suggests creative people will think about case relevance.

Another question arises in this regard: How is this knowledge organized? This issue has been addressed in a study by Mumford et al. (2012). In this study, participants were asked to illustrate their mental models for understanding either a marketing problem or an educational leadership problem – both calling for creative thoughts where judges appraised solution quality, originality, and elegance. It was found that those producing creative problem solutions did not organize knowledge in a novel way but instead organized it such that concepts and cases were structured to permit effective action in problem-solving.

In addition to well-organized knowledge bearing on concepts and cases, people who solve creative problems also evidence a set of higher order, or metacognitive, thinking skills – skills sometimes referred to as cross-process thinking skills. Broadly speaking, it appears that those who produce creative problem solutions evidence five general thinking skills: (1) causal analysis skill, (2) constraint analysis skill, (3) forecasting skill, (4) self-criticism, and (5) wisdom. Marcy and Mumford (2007, 2010) trained people in causal analysis strategies, for example, thinking about causes that have big effects or thinking about causes that have direct effects. They found that training in causal analysis skills resulted in the production of higher quality and more original, as well as more adaptive solutions, in solving creative problems. Medeiros, Partlow, and Mumford (2014) and Medeiros et al. (2018) have shown that skill in analyzing constraints impinging on creative problem-solving also contributes to the production of higher quality, more original, and more elegant problem solutions. Byrne, Shipman, and Mumford (2010) and McIntosh, Mulhearn, and Mumford (2021) have shown that skill in forecasting the downstream implications of process execution also contributes to creative problem-solving.

The importance of self-criticism has been demonstrated in a study by Gibson and Mumford (2013). Here, undergraduates were asked to formulate marketing plans for a clothing firm expanding into a new market. Judges appraised solutions for quality, originality, and elegance. Prior to preparing these plans, however, participants were asked to review and criticize a set of candidate marketing plans. In keeping with the findings of Kozbelt (2007), it was found that those who produced creative problem solutions produced a limited number of deep, thoughtful criticisms. Finally, creative people appear wise, tailoring criticisms and ideas to context and ensuring their solutions are appropriate in this context (Standish, Gujar, & Mumford, under review; Zaccaro et al., 2015).

## 2.3 Who Does This Kind of Work?

The description of creative problem-solving, or creative work, provided earlier in the section, leads to a clear conclusion. Creative work is hard, very hard. Creative people apply experience and substantial expertise, both "book" knowledge and practical experience, in executing multiple processes, where successful execution of each process requires multiple operations, any one of which might fail, and where multiple higher-order thinking skills are required. The substantial cognitive demands made by creative work bring to fore a new question: Who is willing to do this kind of work? In fact, we have a pretty good understanding of the personality of those who are willing to undertake creative work.

Personality is most commonly understood as involving five major personality characteristics: (1) openness, (2) agreeableness, (3) conscientiousness, (4) extraversion, and (5) neuroticism. McCrae (1987) found that the key characteristic evidenced by creative people is openness. Openness refers to behaviors reflecting an engagement with the new or novel – often intellectual, engagement. And, given creative problems require people to work on novel tasks, it is hardly surprising openness has been consistently found to be positively related to both performance in creative problem-solving and real-world creative achievement.

Openness, moreover, is related to two other characteristics evidenced by creative people. First, creative people have a high need for cognition. Creative people like to think about problems, and think about problems in depth. Watts, Steele, and Song (2017) asked undergraduates to solve three different creative problems, all drawn from independent samples, where problem solutions were appraised for quality, originality, and elegance. Need for cognition was measured using Cacioppo, Petty, and Kao's (1984) need for cognition scale. They found that need for cognition was positively related ($r \cong .25$) to the production of high quality, more original, and more elegant solutions across all three creative problems.

Second, openness implies creative people will be curious. Indeed, curiosity about observed anomalies may be critical for information gathering, concept/case selection, and conceptual combination. Hardy, Ness, and Mecca (2017) asked people to complete a measure of curiosity (e.g., find it fascinating to learn new information). Participants were asked to solve a creative marketing problem where judges appraised solution quality and originality. Curiosity was found to be positively related to ($r \cong .25$) to solution quality and originality. Curiosity, however, may be of special significance because it also, along with need for cognition, contributes to ongoing, self-initiated learning – learning likely also to contribute to expertise acquisition.

Introversion, or withdrawing to allow intense, personal processing of environmental cues, has long been linked to creativity, as assessed with respect to both performance on creative problem-solving tasks and real-world creative achievement (McClelland, 1961). In fact, the consistency of this relationship is such that most psychologists assume creative people are inherently introverted – they don't engage others much and they need autonomy (Sheldon, 1995). In Big Five measures, however, extraversion, the opposite of autonomy, examines achievement motives and task engagement. And here, the findings have also been consistent – creative people have strong achievement motives and a focus on getting the work done. Indeed, the finding that psychological disabilities, such as depression and psychoticism, are unrelated to, or negatively related to, real-world achievement (Acar & Runco, 2012; Ramey & Weisberg, 2004) may reflect the need for task focus.

An introverted, autonomous, achievement-oriented person who is open, curious, with a need for cognition is the type of person who will invest in creative work. Feist (1998), however, has asked a somewhat different question about the personality of creative people. More specifically, what do studies comparing creative and noncreative people tell us about their social interactional styles and motives? To answer this question, Feist (1998) conducted a meta-analysis of prior studies comparing more and less creative people working in certain occupational fields. Motivationally, creative people were found to be driven and ambitious. Socially, however, creative people were found to be dominant, arrogant, hostile, self-confident, and autonomous. Put somewhat differently, creative people may not be good team players.

## 2.4 What Environment Do They Work In?

A hostile, dominant, arrogant introvert who is driven and ambitious, open and curious, with a strong need for cognition frames another issue of concern to students of creativity. In what environment will creative people actually get something done? Attempts to answer this question have focused on job design, perceptions of the work environment, feelings about the work environment, and the social context in which the work occurs.

Turning first to job design and the type of tasks that stimulate creative work, Oldham and Cummings (1996) examined the characteristics of tasks that encourage creative problem-solving and eventual creative achievement (e.g., publications, patents). Those working in two manufacturing firms were found to produce their most creative work when the job they were working on was complex, professionally challenging, and they were given adequate autonomy in how to do their work. The need for autonomy and challenge when working through complex tasks implies, however, that creativity cannot occur on all tasks or on all jobs – at least jobs where we limit autonomy, challenge, and complexity.

Studies of creative climate focus on what it is people want in their environment as they work on challenging, complex tasks. In climate studies, people are asked to indicate the extent to which a given attribute of the environment is present (e.g., the resources needed to do my work are available). If people working in a common environment agree, it is assumed this environmental attribute is present. Over the years, a number of climate models have been proposed to account for requisite environmental attributes (e.g., Amabile et al., 1996; Ekvall & Ryhammar, 1999; LaPierre & Giroux, 2003). Hunter, Bedell, and Mumford (2005) reviewed these various models and identified fourteen environmental attributes commonly held to be important for creativity: (1) positive peer group, (2) positive supervisor relationships, (3) resource availability, (4) challenge, (5) mission clarity, (6) autonomy, (7) positive interpersonal exchange, (8) intellectual stimulation, (9) top management support, (10) reward orientation, (11) flexibility and risk-taking, (12) product emphasis, (13) participation, and (14) organizational integration.

Hunter, Bedell, and Mumford (2007) conducted a meta-analysis study to identify the effects of environmental attributes on indices of creative performance such as supervisors' ratings of creativity or publications and patents. They found that climate was strongly positively related to creativity (Cohen's $\Delta$ = .75). Moreover, all these climate attributes were positively related to creativity ($\Delta$ = .51 to .91). However, three environmental attributes were found to be especially strongly related to creativity: (1) positive interpersonal exchange ($\Delta$ = .91), (2) intellectual stimulation ($\Delta$ = .88), and (3) challenge ($\Delta$ = .85). Apparently, a positive, collegial environment characterized by real, significant intellectual challenge is what contributes to creativity. In fact, climate was found to be an especially powerful force shaping creative achievement in competitive, turbulent, and high-pressure institutional settings.

Hunter, Bedell, and Mumford (2007), however, also found that certain characteristics of work teams mediated the impact of climate on creative achievement. Climate was found to exert stronger effects in smaller teams, teams of less than nine people, and teams that evidence only low or moderate cohesion – perhaps because highly cohesive teams reject ideas. In fact, a variety of studies point to a number of team characteristics that also appear to contribute to creative achievement.

First, creativity appears to occur in teams where there is substantial communication both within the team and outside the team to the firm as a whole, the profession, and competitors (Anacona & Caldwell, 1998). Second, teams where all members are encouraged to participate seem to produce more creative products (Zhou, Hirst, & Shipton, 2012). Third, teams that balance the number of creative and noncreative people seem to produce more creative products (Reiter-Palmon, Mitchell, & Royston, 2019) – remember too many cooks can spoil the soufflé! Fourth, creative teams have a depth of task-relevant expertise, often expertise drawn from different, albeit relevant, functional areas (Keller, 2001). Fifth, such teams often position people on the periphery, people with multiple connections to others, to encourage the exchange of diverse, albeit relevant, information (Perry-Smith & Shalley, 2003). Sixth, these teams establish norms to encourage information exchange, evaluation, and work feedback in an open, collegial fashion (Caldwell & O'Reilly, 2003). Seventh, creative teams have adequate, albeit not excessive, resources needed to do the work (Dougherty & Hardy, 1996b; Nohria & Gulati, 1996).

In addition to these structural characteristics of creative teams, they seem to be characterized by feelings of psychological capital among team members: safety to fail, hope, resilience and optimism (Cai et al., 2019). In fact, Amabile and Kramer (2011a), in a qualitative study of more and less successful creative teams, found that creative teams evidence high levels of psychological capital. Mumford and Fichtel (2021) have argued high levels of psychological capital may in fact be required in creative teams as a way of coping with the high risk of failure associated with most forms of creative work.

## 2.5 What Motivates Them?

So, creative people are working on professionally challenging tasks under conditions of intense communication and technical exchange, albeit under conditions where failure is likely. Given these observations, a key question comes to fore: What motivates people to undertake creative work? Amabile (1985) and Hennessey and Amabile (1998) have provided evidence, substantial evidence, which suggests the key force that leads people to invest in creative work is their intrinsic interest in the task itself. Thus, creative people are not, at least completely, motivated by external rewards (e.g., pay, promotions). Instead, interest in the problem, or problems, at hand appears to be the key motivator. What should be recognized here, however, is that intrinsic interest in the problems arising in a domain will contribute to deliberate practice, learning, and expertise acquisition. In fact, a case can be made that the opportunity to learn and develop new knowledge and new skills may be as important a motivator for creative work as their interest in or curiosity about a certain problem.

Although intrinsic motivation is an important force causing people to invest in creative work, this statement should not be taken to imply that creative people have no interest in external rewards. Eisenberger and Shanock (2003) have argued that external rewards may at times motivate creative work. Mumford and Hunter (2005), moreover, have argued that external rewards are noteworthy, in part, because creative people, like most people, want a minimum degree of security, security needed to pursue creative work, and, in part, because external rewards such as pay, promotions, and titles serve to mark status and success.

Professional status and success is, in fact, an important motivator for creative work. Creative people have a strong sense of professional identity, viewing themselves as creative contributors in their profession. In fact, Beghetto and Karwowski (2017) and Karwowski (2011) have provided evidence indicating that a creative self-identity does contribute to people's willingness to invest in solving creative problems. A strong professional identity and a strong identity as a creative professional, however, may contribute to creativity in another way. Those with a strong professional identity and a strong creative identity want to be recognized for creative contributions. And, the desire to be recognized for creative contributions, identity validation, will lead them to seek out and invest substantial effort in addressing creative problems. Indeed, the same forces may be responsible for the finding that competitive pressure, at least up to a point, appears to motivate creative people (Baer et al., 2010).

As important as professional identity and creative identity within a profession are to motivating creative work, to undertake creative work, where the risk of failure is high, creative people need a sense of self-confidence. In keeping with this observation, Tierney and Farmer (2002) and Tierney, Farmer, and Graen (1999) developed a measure of creative self-efficacy. They found, in a study of chemists, not only that creative self-efficacy contributed to supervisory evaluations of creative achievement, publications, and invention disclosures, it also made a unique contribution in accounting for creative achievement above and beyond general job self-efficacy.

Beyond creative self-efficacy, a creative professional identity, and intrinsic interest in the problem at hand, creative people seem to evidence two other characteristics that serve to motivate creative work. Furnham (2020) conducted a qualitative, observational study of creative professionals. He found that creative work was motivated by two key variables. The first variable was persistent engagement in the problem. The second variable was obsession: intense, ongoing investment in thinking about the problem.

## 2.6 Do Leaders Have a Problem?

A persistent, obsessive person who is confident and has a strong sense of professional identity with an interest only in those problems they feel are important is not an easy person to manage. Although creative people want to accomplish something, a dominant, hostile, arrogant, and critical person is certainly not the ideal employee we commonly seek in firms. To make matters even worse, these same characteristics of creative people will make it difficult for them to work with others – to work in teams. It is in teams, however, that most creative work occurs in real-world settings. Thus, the fundamental personality and motivation of creative people makes them a "difficult" group to manage.

To complicate matters even further, the work they are being asked to do is daunting. They are being asked to produce a high-quality, original, and elegant solution to a complex, novel, ill-defined problem. To produce these solutions they must execute multiple processing operations, where each process is a complex operation on its own right and the likelihood of failure is high. Expertise, both "book" and "bench" expertise, is needed to solve these kinds of problems. And, to have any hope of solving these kinds of problems, substantial motivation, self-confidence, and a strong personal sense of professional engagement is, in fact, required.

But how are we to get these people to work together? How are we to get them to engage in problems of interest to the firm, not just those problems they find intrinsically, professionally interesting? How can firms "use" the many failures likely to be encountered in creative work? A firm's ability to answer these and a host of other questions broached by the nature of creative people and creative work ultimately depends on the quality of those asked to lead creative efforts for the firm.

## 3 Leading Creative People

When one considers the concerns of institutions with respect to innovation, and the nature of creative work, it is not surprising that many firms stay away from creative efforts. Nonetheless, at least some firms do seek innovation due to basic business strategy. Moreover, for these firms, innovation is the key to growth, profits, and survival. By the same token, however, firms must deal with the direct and indirect costs associated with any new innovation: costs that, at times, may disrupt basic operations. Not only are firms keenly aware of the costs of innovation, they are also keenly aware that innovative efforts often fail. And, to make matters worse, they may not even recognize, or be able to develop, the best ideas presented.

The uncertainty associated with innovation is further compounded by the nature of the people who must produce the creative ideas that provide the basis for innovation. These tend to be hostile and domineering people whose concern is not the success and survival of the firm. Instead, their key concern is, albeit not entirely, advancement in their professional field. And, while development of any creative idea into an innovative product requires teamwork, these are not people who work especially well with others. To make matters even worse, their concern is likely to be focused on the *idea* per se, rather than the practical development of the idea. This is especially true when development of the idea requires working with people from other professions who have a different "language" and different concerns.

What we have here is a mess, an institution uncertain about perusing an innovation that must rely on difficult people to make the innovation "real." These observations bring to fore a fundamental question. How can institutions manage the firm, and the creative people working in the firm, to form viable creative ideas into successful innovative products? Although there are many potential answers to this question, it seems clear that effective leadership of both the firm and creative people working in the firm is one key mechanism for answering this question (Mumford et al., 2018, 2020).

## 3.1 What Is Leadership?

We all have an image, an often highly stereotypical image, of what is meant by the term leadership or leader. Although we typically see leaders as heroic figures (e.g., Franklin Roosevelt, John F. Kennedy, Martin Luther King) (Meindl, 1995), this image, however evocative, is simply not correct. Leadership is defined as the exercise of influence so as to change the behaviors, beliefs, or values of others (Bass & Bass, 2008; Yukl, 2011). It should be recognized here that what is critical to leadership is the exercise of influence – influence exercised either for good or bad with respect to people, teams, or firms.

Often we assume that leaders exercise influence with respect to people. In order to successfully do so, leaders must communicate (Baker & Ganster, 1985) and build a sense of trust in others (Braun et al., 2013). Although direct interaction with others often provides a basis for the exercise of influence, it is not an absolute requirement. As Mumford et al. (2000) note, influence may be exercised through many mechanisms – often mechanisms that do not require direct contact with others. For example, setting budgets has a noteworthy impact on peoples' behavior in firms, but budget setting does not require direct interpersonal contact.

Leadership, moreover, is a phenomenon that occurs in a defined social role. Within firms we typically assume leadership occurs in managerial roles (Fleishman et al., 1991). The importance of roles is evident in a distinction drawn between leader emergence, gaining access to a leadership role, and leader performance, or the effective exercise of influence in this role. What must be recognized here, however, is that when we speak of leader performance, we are referring to how well the person holding the role performed with respect to the demands faced by occupants of this *specific* role. Thus, in studying leadership we typically distinguish between key types of roles, such as formal or informal leadership roles, or alternatively, top management versus middle management. What should be recognized here, however, is that leadership of creative efforts can occur in many roles – any role where others (i.e., followers, teams, firms, stakeholders) value creativity and innovation. Thus, creative leadership is not limited to research and development efforts, as it may occur in manufacturing, logistics, and purchasing as well.

## 3.2 Does Leadership Make a Difference?

Our foregoing observations are noteworthy because they bring to fore another question: Does effective leadership, in leadership roles where creativity is valued in firms, contribute to generation of creative problem solutions and the development and implementation of innovative new products? Studies of leader behavior, behavior as perceived by the leader, their followers, or their superiors, have all indicated that effective leadership is a powerful influence contributing to both creativity and subsequent innovation.

In one study along these lines, Keller (2006) assessed the performance of 118 research and development project teams with respect to outcomes such as the technical quality of their work, schedule performance, cost performance, and speed to market – all criteria used to assess the success of innovative efforts (Thamhain, 2011). He assessed the extent to which leaders exhibited structuring behavior, such as defining team goals, obtaining requisite resources, providing work plans, and delivering performance feedback, based on followers' appraisals of leader behavior. Results indicated that leader structuring behavior was positively correlated in the .30s with these innovation criteria. Along similar lines, Barnowe (1975) found that leader structuring behaviors, especially when accompanied by technical skill, were positively related ($r \approx .40$) to indices of creativity (e.g., senior managers appraisals) and innovation (e.g., publications) among some 963 chemists working in research and development departments.

Tierney, Farmer, and Graen (1999) examined the impact of another form of leader behavior on creativity and innovation: positive interpersonal exchange relationships between leaders and followers. They assessed the number of invention disclosures filed and senior managers' appraisals of creativity among 191 research and development employees in a chemical firm. It was found that positive exchange relationships between leaders and followers were positively related, in the mid-30s, to invention disclosures and managerial appraisals of employee creativity. Other studies by Atwater and Carmeli (2009), Lee (2008), and Qu, Janssen, and Shi (2015) also point to the impact of positive leader follower exchange on employee creativity and innovation.

Not only is leader-structuring behavior and positive leader member exchange related to creativity and innovation, transformational leadership behaviors have also been found to be positively related to creativity and innovation. Transformational leadership subsumes four dimensions: (1) inspiration, (2) idealized motivation, (3) intellectual stimulation, and (4) individualized consideration (Bass, 1997). Shin and Zhou (2003) examined the relationship between transformational leadership and creativity among 290 followers. Creativity was assessed using managerial appraisals of follower creativity. Followers appraised the transformational behaviors of their leaders. It was found that leaders who exhibited more transformational behaviors had followers who exhibited greater creativity ($r = .22$). Eisenbeiss and Boerner (2013) also obtained a positive relationship between leaders' transformational behavior and the creativity of 416 research and development employees. Other work by Jaussi and Dionne (2003) has shown that transformational leadership contributes to creative problem-solving – the production of higher quality and more original solutions to creative problems. Again, the relationships obtained in these studies indicate a relationship in the range of .30 to .40.

Of course, many models of desirable leadership behavior in addition to initiating structure, leader member exchange, and transformational leadership have been proposed over the years. And many of these behaviors, for example, the behaviors expressed by authentic leaders (e.g. Černe, Jaklič, & Škerlavaj, 2013), servant leaders (e.g. Yoshida et al., 2014), and benevolent leaders (e.g. Wang & Cheng, 2010), have all been found to be positively related to creativity and innovation. The many studies demonstrating a strong, positive relationship between leader behavior and follower creativity and innovation, of course, cry out for a general summary of these findings.

Hughes et al. (2018) conducted a review of the some 195 studies examining the relationship between leader behavior and follower creativity and innovation. They distinguished between criterion measures focused on follower creativity (e.g., managerial ratings of follower creativity) and innovation (e.g., publications, patents, market growth with new product introductions). They found that leader member exchange, empowering leadership, and servant leadership behaviors were all strongly, positively related, $r > .30$, $r < .50$, to both creativity and innovation criteria. Thus, it appears that leadership, at least certain forms of leadership behavior, is strongly, positively related to both creativity and innovation in "real world" settings. Indeed, the strength of these relationships is such that they suggest effective leadership may be key to creativity and innovation in firms.

## 3.3 How Do Leaders Impact Creativity and Innovation?

The impact of leader structuring behavior on creativity and innovation (Keller, 2006) has an important, albeit often overlooked, implication. More specifically, this implies that one way leaders shape creative work is through planning. Plans, plans disseminated to teams, allow people to coordinate their efforts while discussing, developing, and executing creative ideas. Some support for this proposition may be found in a study by Marta, Leritz, and Mumford (2005).

In the Marta, Leritz, and Mumford (2005) study, participants were asked to work as a team of consultants formulating plans for turning around a failing automotive firm. Teams' written plans were appraised by judges for quality and originality. After completing their plans, team members nominated their leaders. And, before starting work on these plans, all team members were asked to complete a measure of planning skills. It was found that the most creative turnaround plans were produced when the team was led by someone with strong planning skills.

Planning, of course, is a complex cognitive activity (Mumford, Schultz, & Van Doorn, 2001). Thus, the viability of the plans formulated by leaders will depend on the leader possessing a number of other key skills. For example, Shipman, Byrne, and Mumford (2010) have shown that leader forecasting skills contribute to the formation of viable plans. Marcy and Mumford (2010) have shown that the formation of viable plans also depends on the leader's ability to identify critical causes. Still, other work by Medeiros et al. (2018) has shown that leader skill in identifying key constraints impinging on plan execution is also of some importance.

The fact that transformational leadership contributes to creativity and innovation (Gumusluoglu & Ilsev, 2009) suggests another way that leader behavior might influence creativity and innovation. One key aspect of transformational leadership is intellectual stimulation. And, intellectually challenging people has been found to be a key dimension of the kind of climate contributing to creativity and innovation (Hunter, Bedell, & Mumford, 2007). Accordingly, Boies, Fiset, and Gill (2015) conducted an experimental study where forty-four teams were asked to produce creative products. Notably, manipulations were made in the behavior of confederate leaders such that intellectual stimulation was, or was not, provided through behaviors such as asking about basic approach or encouraging the team not to underestimate task difficulty. And, it was found that leader intellectual stimulation contributed to team creativity. More broadly, these findings indicate that leader behavior may be a powerful force shaping the kinds of work climate likely to encourage creativity.

Additional direct support for the impact of leader behavior in shaping the kind of climate contributing to creativity has been provided by Khalili (2016). In this study, participants' creativity was appraised by managers. In addition, participants were asked to describe their supervisors with respect to the key dimensions of transformational leadership and whether their work environment evidenced a creative climate. Results indicated that the impact of transformational leadership on follower creativity was mediated through creative climate. Thus, leader behavior does seem to establish a work environment that followers see as supporting creativity.

Leaders' impact on climate, however, may not be the only way leaders encourage creativity and innovation. Creativity, as noted earlier, requires people to work through complex, novel, and ill-defined problems. As a result, creativity requires knowledge sharing and ongoing learning. In this regard, a study by Dong et al. (2017) is of some importance. They asked the supervisors of forty-three research and development teams to appraise team creativity. In addition, participants described the transformational behaviors exhibited by their supervisors along with knowledge sharing within the team, and individual skill development (i.e., learning). It was found that the impact of transformational leadership on creativity was mediated through follower knowledge sharing and skill development. Thus, leaders, by encouraging people to think and learn as they work through creative problems, can contribute to subsequent creative performance.

It has, in fact, long been recognized that a key role played by leaders of creative efforts is encouraging participation in creative efforts by all team members (Maier & Solem, 1970). This "old" observation has been confirmed in a more recent study by Nijstad, Berger-Selman, and De Dreu (2014). They studied thirty-six top management teams where production of radical innovations was assessed. Team members appraised senior leaders' transformational behavior as well as team members willingness to dissent. They found that team members' willingness to voice dissenting views and active participation contributed to firm innovation, and that voicing dissent was encouraged by transformational leaders.

Nijstad, Berger-Selman, and De Dreu (2014), however, also found that the effects of transformational leadership depended in part on followers feeling they were safe to voice dissent – participative safety. Amabile and Kramer (2011b) conducted a qualitative study of creative information technology teams. They found that to the extent leaders provided support to followers and induced feelings of psychological safety, creativity was more likely to be observed. Some support for this observation has been provided by Carmeli, Reiter-Palmon, and Ziv (2010). In this study, leader inclusiveness was assessed by some 150 research and development employees. In addition, participants reported feelings of psychological safety and psychological capital while indicating engagement in creative work. They found that inclusive leadership induced feelings of psychological safety, which, in turn, contributed to engagement in creative work.

Of course, psychological safety and psychological capital may be induced by other forms of leader behavior. For example, trust in the leader brought about by leader authenticity may contribute to investment in creative work and eventual creative achievement (Rego et al., 2014). Psychological capital and creativity may also be encouraged by the support leaders provide for creative work – anticipating its value and providing requisite resources. In keeping with this observation, Eisenbeiss, Van Knippenberg, and Boerner (2008) found that transformational leadership contributes to support for innovation, and in an appropriate climate, support for innovation contributes to employee creativity among the members of thirty-three research and development teams.

However, it may not be enough for leaders to support creativity and innovation in general. They may also need to support the individuals doing creative work. Tierney and Farmer (2002) found that creative self-efficacy, confidence in one's ability to do creative work, contributes to creative achievement. Tierney, Farmer, and Graen (1999) found that creative self-efficacy arises in part as a function of positive interpersonal exchange relationships between leaders and their followers. Thus, leaders by building a sense of creative self-confidence in their followers can stimulate creative work and innovative contributions. Indeed, as leaders serve as role models, a leader's sense of creative self-efficacy and their personal involvement in creative work may build feelings of creative self-efficacy in followers and encourage follower involvement in creative work (Zhao & Guo, 2019).

Leaders, of course, do not just interact with individual followers; leaders also establish normative work practices. Normative work practices such as knowledge sharing expectations, valuing expertise, and a focus on technical rather than personal criticism, all contribute to creative achievement (Ford, 1996). One critical variable in this regard is team reflexivity, or a team's ongoing appraisal of its work processes and the outcomes of team actions. Schippers, West, and Dawson (2015) have shown that team reflexivity, in fact, contributes to innovation in a study of ninety-eight health care teams. Maccurtain et al. (2009) examined reflexivity among the leaders of thirty-nine software firms. They found that the reflexivity of top management teams was positively related to the success of new product development efforts. Not only does a leader encouragement of team reflexivity contribute to innovation, it may also encourage dissent, participation, and creative self-efficacy (De Dreu, 2002). Thus, leaders by encouraging teams to learn, and establishing norms supporting learning and reflexivity, may make a noteworthy contribution to follower creativity and subsequent innovative achievement.

Of course, teams do not exist in an isolated environment; they exist in the context of a broader organizational environment. And, Dougherty and Hardy (1996a) found that institutional support for creative efforts, support provided by top management, was critical to the successful fielding of innovative new products. Top management support, however, for reasons noted earlier, is not guaranteed. Thus, the leaders of creative efforts must champion the creative effort to build institutional support (Markham & Smith, 2017). In fact, Lu et al. (2019) found that leaders must be skilled in upward influence tactics, and viable demonstrations of the *potentiality* of creative ideas, if they are to garner the support needed from the firm.

## 3.4 What Must Leaders Do?

Leadership has a number of effects on followers and teams that make creativity and innovation possible. Leaders plan and structure work activities. They establish a climate needed to encourage engagement in creative work. They help build a sense of psychological safety and confidence in one's creative capacity. They establish team norms and processes likely to support creativity. And, they obtain the institutional support needed for creative work. Although all of these observations are important, they all refer to how a leader's behavior is perceived by others. Thus, these studies do not directly speak to what the leader themselves, must do when leading creative work. Put differently, what are the key functions, or activities, leaders of creative efforts must be able to execute (Fleishman et al., 1991; Mumford et al., 2000)?

Robledo, Peterson, and Mumford (2012) proposed a general model describing the key functions, or activities, that must be executed by those asked to lead creative efforts. This model assumes that leaders must execute key functions with respect to three vectors or domains of action. In keeping with much of the work on the relationship between leader behaviors (e.g., transformational leadership, leader member exchange) and follower creativity, they argue that leaders must manage and facilitate the team, and individual members of the team, as they engage in creative efforts – the group vector. They argued, however, that leaders' interactions with the team are contingent on the content of the work to be done – the work vector. In creative efforts, however, it is not enough just to lead the team and the work. The firm must understand and support the work being done – support that is not just top management approval but also the active engagement of other critical functional areas in the firm. Thus, the third key vector in the model is leading the organization. Within each of these three vectors of leader activities are a number, a rather large number, of discrete functional activities that must be executed by the leader. For example, to lead the firm leaders must: (1) acquire resources, (2) build support among other relevant units, and (3) import appropriate expertise and technology at the right time. Figure 2 presents the key functional activities leaders must execute to lead the work, lead the group, and lead the organization.

Of course, presentation of a model of this sort begs a question: Is there empirical support for this model? Vessey et al. (2014) have provided some rather compelling evidence for the viability of this model of leader functional activities. This study was based on a series of key benchmark cases – specifically eminent scientists and engineers who have led multiple creative efforts: creative efforts that not only resulted in the development of new concepts but also the development of new technologies – scientists such as Robert Oppenheimer (physics, nuclear technology), Francis Crick (microbiology, DNA structure), and Lee De Forest (electronics, television). In all, some ninety-three eminent scientists and engineers for whom academic biographies that

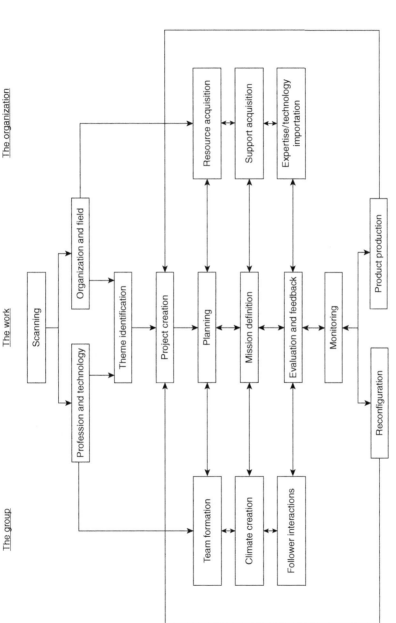

**Figure 2** Model of leadership proposed by Robledo, Peterson, and Mumford (2012)

were validated, and positively reviewed, were identified – under the constraint the scientist or engineer of interest was active after 1920 and the biography had been written after 1950.

Two psychologists then reviewed each biography to identify incidents where the scientist or engineer of interest evidenced leadership – influence over others. Descriptions of these leadership events ranged from a paragraph to ten pages in length with roughly thirty-five pages of leadership events being identified for each scientist and engineer. Three judges, all doctoral students familiar with the leadership literature, were asked to rate each identified leadership event with respect to the key constructs embedded in the model of creative leadership activities described earlier (e.g., clarifying mission, obtaining support, establishing creative climate). This panel of judges had good agreement, $r_{tt}$ = .79, in appraising leadership with respect to these variables.

In addition, judges reviewed the summary sections of biographies, typically the introductory or conclusion chapters, to identify markers of their performance and the h-index of these scientists and engineers was obtained. These criteria included, in addition to the h-index, dyadic influence, group influence, organizational influence, field influence, public policy influence, theoretical influence, technical influence, number of creative products produced, number of major professional awards, and number of groups or organizations led. In addition, judges coded a number of covariate controls such as book length, author's liking of the leader, event detail, and strength of documentation.

A factor analysis identified five key dimensions of performance: (1) technical influence, (2) professional influence, (3) team leadership, (4) team performance, and (5) theoretical influence. Of greater importance, however, was the finding that technical influence, professional influence, and team leadership were found to be strongly positively related to effective execution of these functional leadership activities ($r$ = .40–.60). Thus, the three-vector model describing the key functional requirements of those asked to lead creative efforts does seem to account for performance differences among eminent scientists and engineers.

Although not all leaders of creative efforts lead teams that make creative contributions of the scope that results in a biography focusing on their career, these are model cases for the effective leadership of creative efforts. And, Robledo, Peterson, and Mumford (2012) seem to have provided a viable account for how these people led creative efforts. Accordingly, in the following sections we will examine what we know about leading the work, leading the group or team, and leading the organization or firm.

## 4 Leading the Work

The model of creative leadership proposed by Robledo, Peterson, and Mumford (2012), a model validated by Vessey et al. (2014), stresses the importance of leading the work. Although all leaders must, at least to some extent, exercise influence with respect to accomplishing the work, work-oriented leadership takes on special significance for those asked to lead creative efforts. The significance of leading the work, however, is not especially surprising when one considers the nature of creativity and the characteristics of the people willing to tackle creative projects.

Earlier we noted creative work involves problem-solving – solving complex, novel, and ill-defined, or poorly structured, problems (Mumford & Gustafson, 2007) using expertise as well as a complex set of problem-solving skills. To solve complex, novel, ill-defined problems, however, some structure must be imposed – typically structure imposed by a leader (Barnowe, 1975; Keller, 2006). In fact, it is difficult to see how, or why, institutions would support creative efforts, given the costs and risks associated with such efforts, if a viable structure for the work had not been provided.

The need for structure in leading the work is not, however, solely a matter of objective work conditions. Earlier, we also noted that creative people are hostile, autonomous, domineering, critical people focused on achievement in their own profession (Feist, 1998). Creative work in institutions, however, typically occurs in teams. And, these are not people who are especially amenable to teamwork or, for that matter, people from different professional fields – people who are needed to develop creative ideas into viable, innovative, new products. Without a leader's imposition of structure on the work, it is difficult to see how viable new products would ever emerge from creative teams.

## 4.1 Why Scanning and Themes?

The foundation for a leader's successful direction of the work is ultimately the leader's expertise with respect to the professional field and the role of the professional field in the firm. This rather straightforward point is underscored in an older study examining when and why creative people will accept influence and direction from others. Thamhain and Gemmill (1974) examined the effects of the influence tactics used by leaders (e.g., reward, coercion) on research and development personnel's appraisal of managerial effectiveness. They found only one influence tactic, expertise, resulted in positive appraisals of leader effectiveness. The importance of leader expertise is not simply an issue of what followers want – remember, creative people are professionally focused; thus, it is also related to the activities leaders must execute.

Leaders must gather information to direct the work. Thus, Kickul and Gundry (2001) have shown that the performance of those asked to lead creative efforts in firms depends on the intensity and accuracy of their ongoing information-gathering activities – activities referred to as scanning. Given the need to structure technical work, it is not surprising that leaders of creative efforts intensely scan advances in the external, technical environment (Allen & Cohen, 1969). In a recent qualitative study of leaders of creative groups working in technology firms, Amabile et al. (2004) found information gathering to be a key leader activity. What should be remembered here, however, is that leaders gather information not only from the profession but also the institution in which they are working – what problems and capabilities does the firm have?

Scanning the profession and scanning the firm, however, both require expertise. Expertise not only tells people what information is important, it also provides strategies and contacts for more effective information gathering. Thus, experts know what technical journals to keep up with and can process the information provided by those journals with greater ease and greater accuracy while also being able to see the downstream implications of this information (Mumford et al., 2009). Expertise and exposure, however, also allow leaders to establish networks of contacts – contacts in both the profession and the firm. And, the establishment of rich networks of contacts with both the firm and the profession appears to contribute to the effective leadership of creative efforts. Indeed, the leaders of creative efforts seem to spend substantial time and resources both building and exploiting these networks (Gertner, 2012).

The information gathering through extensive, ongoing, scanning activities by leaders is of special importance because it provides a basis for theme identification. Leaders cannot define projects willy-nilly. There must be some organization to the creative projects being pursued by a firm. An organized set of creative projects provides firms not only with staff who have relevant expertise, it also provides firms with a framework for learning from project work. The themes leaders seek to pursue are typically defined with respect to a certain limited set of fundamentals (Hughes, 1989). Thus, DuPont focused its creative work on the properties of long-chain polymers (Hounshell, 1992) while Bell labs focused its creative work on the clarity and management of long-distance telecommunications (Gertner, 2012).

Fundamentals that must be defined by leaders, however, are complex – too complex unto themselves to effectively guide project work. Thus, leaders must identify a limited number of themes, with respect to a fundamental, on which creative teams will be asked to work. What should be recognized here, however, is these themes must represent an integrated set such that what is learned with respect to one of them will contribute to work on other themes.

Thus, Root-Bernstein, Bernstein, and Garnier (1995) found that scientific leaders and Nobel Prize winners leading significant laboratories typically focused their work, and their project teams, on three to five integrated themes.

These observations, however, broach another question: Exactly how do leaders of creative efforts identify viable themes? One answer to this question pertains to the leaders' understanding, or the leaders' sensemaking, of the field and firm in which they are working. Thus, Andersen, Barker, and Chen (2006) argued that the mental models leaders construct, models that specify key causes and outcomes, are critical to technical, scientific leadership. In keeping with this observation, Mumford et al. (2012) taught people to illustrate their mental models of creative problems. They found that people who had more accurate mental models focusing on a limited number of key causes produced more creative solutions to leadership and marketing problems calling for creative thought. Moreover, in another series of studies, Marcy and Mumford (2007, 2010) have shown that people who are especially skilled at identifying key causes, causes that operate to determine the behavior of complex systems, are those most likely to produce creative problem solutions.

Theme identification, however, is not simply a matter of mental models and use of these mental models to identify critical causes. Leaders must think about how these themes will unfold over time. Put differently, leaders of creative efforts must think downstream or be able to forecast the implications of pursuing given themes. Some support for this observation has been provided in a qualitative study conducted by O'Connor (1998). She interviewed eight leaders who had directed projects resulting in successful radical innovations. It was that found these leaders were able to envision, or forecast, the long-term implications of work on a given theme for both the profession and the firm.

In fact, empirical studies have provided some support for this proposition. In studies by Byrne, Shipman, and Mumford (2010) and Shipman, Byrne, and Mumford (2010), people were asked to provide solutions to an educational leadership problem or a marketing leadership problem – both problems calling for creative thought. As people worked on these tasks, they were asked to forecast the implications of pursuing ideas. Judges appraised various attributes of these forecasts and it was found, in forecasting, that four key dimensions were evident: (1) the extensiveness of forecasts, (2) forecasting time frame, (3) forecasting resource requirements, and (4) forecasting potential negative outcomes. In was found that those who produced original, high-quality, and elegant solutions to these problems forecasted more extensively and over longer time frames. In a later study, McIntosh, Mulhearn, and Mumford (2021) found that those who forecasted both the positive and the negative outcomes produced the most creative problem solutions.

## 4.2 How to Define Projects and Project Plans?

Leader forecasting is noteworthy because it tells us about how leaders define projects and specify the project work to be undertaken by teams. To begin, leaders will use their mental models, and the key causes, both known and suspected causes, to identify the projects in a thematic area that might be worth pursuing. And, it appears leaders consider a relatively wide array of projects that might be worth pursuing. Leaders, however, will also forecast the implications of pursuing project work with respect to both the profession and the firm, with high payoff projects that might contribute to both the profession and the firm being those they pursue. Thus, forecasts provide the basis for the projects that will be pursued by those leading creative efforts.

Forecasts, however, are not just a tool for identifying what projects to pursue. Forecasts allow leaders to establish constraints bearing on the project at hand – how much time, how much money, what limitations on the technology or process. With the definition of constraints leaders have begun to define the context in which a project might be conducted – project creation.

Traditionally, it has been assumed that constraints inhibit creative thought and, thus, the success of innovative efforts. If you constrain creative people, you limit their ability to come up with new ideas. For the leaders of creative efforts, however, identification of constraints will prove critical. First, some constraints cannot be satisfied or worked around. Thus, the project is "dead" before it has begun. Second, constraints provide a mechanism for structuring and directing the creative work of others without imposing a need for the overly close supervision which has been found to disrupt creative work. The leader need only specify that all work done must be within these constraints. Third, identification of potential constraints serves to identify key issues that must be addressed by the leader and/or the team in pursuing project work.

Moreover, identification of key constraints does not, in fact, appear to inhibit creativity and innovation. Instead, it appears to provide a framework for, and a stimulus to, creative thought. For example, Kidder (1981), in a qualitative study of innovation in the computer sciences, found that a leader's imposition of an appropriate set of key constraints on a project team was a crucial, perhaps the one crucial, determinant of successful introduction of a new product. And, in recent years, empirical support has begun to be gathered that supports the value of constraint imposition on creative work.

In one study along these lines, Medeiros, Partlow, and Mumford (2014) asked undergraduates, some 300 in all, to develop advertising campaigns for a new product, a high-energy root beer, where judges appraised the quality, originality, and elegance of the resulting advertising campaigns. As participants worked on their campaigns, they received "emails" from their putative supervisor who established constraints with respect to marketing fundamentals, marketing themes, marketing environment, and marketing objectives. It was found that established constraints with respect to marketing objectives resulted in the production of more creative advertising campaigns, especially when participants were highly motivated.

In another study along these lines, Medeiros et al. (2018) asked some 300 undergraduates to provide a business plan for a new restaurant chain – plans appraised by judges for quality, originality, and elegance. As people worked through this task, they were asked to answer questions about key thinking processes (e.g., problem definition, conceptual combination, idea generation, idea evaluation). And, prior to providing their answers to these questions, constraints were imposed. It was found that the most creative restaurant plans were obtained when constraints were imposed early on during problem definition.

The importance of defining constraints in project creation points to a key skill needed by leaders of creative efforts. Leaders of creative efforts need exceptional problem definition skills (Redmond, Mumford, & Teach, 1993). Mumford et al. (1996) assessed the strategies contributing to effective problem definition by examining the type of information used in problem definition and its contribution to creative problem-solving. They found that those who produced creative problem solutions defined problems with respect to constraints and procedures, not goals. And, effective problem definition based on constraints and procedures was found to be strongly, positively, related to subsequent performance in solving creative problems. Thus, problem definition and constraint identification in problem definition are likely to be critical to the successful leadership of creative efforts.

With project creation and constraint identification, leaders can begin to plan how work on a project will be conducted. In fact, project planning seems to be the key skill required of those asked to lead creative efforts. Hemlin (2009) studied the leaders of eighty-four research groups working in universities and for-profit bio-technology firms. He found that the leaders of creative teams were willing to delegate many of their work activities with one exception: project planning. Put quite directly, leaders of creative efforts see project planning as their critical key activity.

Mumford, Mecca, and Watts (2015) have described the key activities that must be executed by people in formulating plans. They begin by noting that plans are formulated using case-based, or experiential, knowledge – a complex form of knowledge where information is stored about causes, resources, restrictions, contingencies, actions, goals, actor affect, and systems (Kolodner, 1997).

This case-based knowledge is used to form a local mental model for understanding the task at hand. And, this local mental model is used to forecast the key actions required in sequence along with the formation of backup plans that might need to be executed under certain contingencies. Indeed, plans allow not only for organized, efficient action, they also induce action flexibility by allowing people to identify unexpected, emergent opportunities (Patalano & Seifert, 1997).

In fact, the evidence accrued over the years points to the impact of leader planning on creativity. For example, in one study along these lines, Marta, Leritz, and Mumford (2005) asked teams to work on a corporate turnaround plan, where turnaround plans were appraised by judges for quality and originality. Prior to starting work on these plans, the planning skills of all team members were assessed. After completing their plans, team members were also asked to nominate their leaders. It was found that the most creative turnarounds were produced by teams whose leader's evidenced strong planning skills. In another study along these lines, Osburn and Mumford (2006) asked participants to formulate plans for leading a new experimental school where judges appraised plan quality and originality. Notably, participants were, or were not, given instruction bearing on key planning skills. And, it was found that those given instruction in planning skills produced stronger, more creative plans for leading this experimental school.

Not only do leader planning skills influence performance, how leaders plan also makes a difference. In one study along these lines, Caughron and Mumford (2008) asked participants to solve three educational problems calling for creative thought. Judges appraised the quality, originality, and elegance of the resulting problem solutions. Before starting work on these tasks, however, participants were, or were not, asked to apply three planning techniques: (1) Gantt charts, (2) case-based planning, or (3) critical path analysis where key obstacles/contingencies on plan execution were laid out. They found that critical path analysis contributed to the production of more creative problem solutions, presumably because it promotes the management of obstacles and contingencies in plan execution. In another study along these lines, Giorgini and Mumford (2013) asked participants to formulate plans for restructuring a firm, which judges appraised for quality, originality, and elegance. Participants were also asked to form backup plans, which were appraised for depth and detail. They found that those producing stronger backup plans also produced more creative problem solutions, especially when they were primed to think about resource requirements for plan execution.

For those leading creative efforts, however, planning may prove especially complicated. Mumford, Bedell-Avers, and Hunter (2008) proposed a model of the planning activities occurring in firms seeking to field innovative new products (see Figure 3). They described leader planning activities with respect to the stage of project work, scanning or exploration, template planning or critical technical development, prototyping, production, and fielding. In this model, projects based on different themes are being pursued at different stages of development. What is of note is that the key issues of concern in project work, and the critical issues of concern, shift as a project moves from exploration to fielding. Moreover, projects become less technical based and more organizationally based with idea development. And, they become both better organized and more complex, involving more functional units, and where the establishment of cross-functional teams will be required as efforts move from initial exploration to fielding new products.

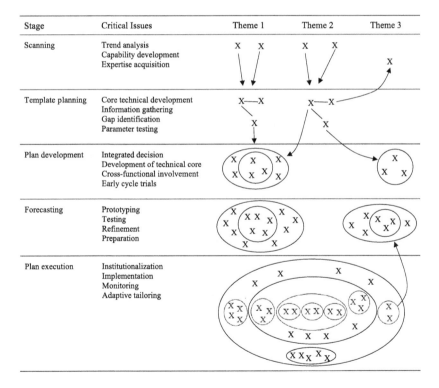

Note. X = Project elements

○ = Indicate more or less tightly integrated elements

⟶ = Indicate movement of or incorporation of elements

**Figure 3** Planning model proposed by Mumford, Bedell-Avers, and Hunter (2008)

This model is noteworthy for understanding leader planning activities for six reasons. First, leader planning activities are ongoing with plans being reconfigured as work on projects progresses. Second, the success of work on a plan must be evaluated with respect to different criteria depending on the stage of project development. Third, leaders may give up on their plans, and eliminate work executing these plans, for different reasons at different points in project development. Fourth, more expertise, and different forms of expertise must be integrated into project teams as projects proceed to fielding. Fifth, critical issues, constraints, and obstacles will change as projects proceed. Six, leaders and teams must learn at each stage of plan execution. Thus, plans provide a framework for learning as well as project execution. These observations are noteworthy because they imply leaders of creative efforts must not only plan well, their planning must also be dynamic and flexible.

## 4.3 How Are Plans Made Real?

Leaders, necessarily, must communicate plans to their followers. And, in fact, traditional communication skills, clarity, brevity, delineating stakeholder interest, are all needed by those asked to lead creative efforts. In communicating plans to followers, however, leaders must also help followers make sense of, or understand, the intent and implications of their plans. In fact, Hill and Levenhagen (1995) have argued that effective sensemaking on the part of leaders is critical to the success of innovative efforts in firms. People must see how plans will unfold and the significance of the plan. Some rather compelling support for this proposition has been provided in a study by Dougherty et al. (2000). In this study, interviews were conducted with principals working in innovative and noninnovative firms. They found that in innovative firms, future paths, key skills, available resources, and absorption of emerging trends into the firm were explicitly stressed in leader sensemaking.

Shin, Yuan, and Zhou (2017) note, however, that the impact of leader sensemaking in mission definition also depends on leaders explicitly articulating the nature of creative work that will be required of followers. In fact, those leading creative efforts typically stress, in mission definition, the nature of the creative work required but also key contingencies impinging on how this work is to be accomplished. Thus, leaders' analysis and definition of constraints in project creation provides one key type of information to be provided to followers in mission definition.

Leaders in mission definition, however, must provide a number of other types of information to guide creative work. Some of the information provided is factual: what resources are available, what skills are available or must be developed, and who are the key players both within and outside the institution. Some of the information leaders must provide in mission definition and sense-making, however, is less concrete and more social: for example, what is a key evaluation criteria, how will evaluation occur as the project proceeds, what are institutional expectations, and how might the project, if successful, contribute to the firm and the relevant professional fields? Leaders, moreover, will often find it useful to describe the linkages between various projects, and the nature of the creative work required on these projects, to help followers make sense of the project at hand (Dougherty et al., 2000).

In defining missions and helping followers make sense of the work they are being asked to do, leaders must take into account the nature of their followers and the conditions likely to motivate them to invest in creative work. One key issue in this regard is that leaders must build in followers a sense of creative self-efficacy, expressing confidence in their ability to complete the creative work called for (Tierney & Farmer, 2002). Another issue that should be borne in mind is the focus of creative people on professional achievement. Thus, in mission definition, the contributions of the work to the profession and/or development of requisite professional skills should be described. Finally, the leader should expressly articulate the importance of the work, in part, to focus criticism on technical as opposed to personal issues, and, in part, to provide an overarching shared sense of mission which will encourage autonomous, dominant, and hostile people to work together.

Ultimately, in mission definition, leaders should seek to build a shared mental model among followers concerning the nature and significance of the work. In fact, Davison and Blackman (2005) and Lee-Kelley and Blackman (2005) have argued the availability of shared mental models with respect to the work to be accomplished is a critical force shaping the performance of creative teams. And, in fact, Mumford et al. (2001), in an experimental study, found that induction of shared mental models contributed to creative performance of teams working to solve problems calling for creative thought.

## 4.4 How Do You Appraise Work with Respect to Plans?

Farris (1972) examined the conditions under which creative people, research and development scientists, sought feedback from their leaders. He found that creative people sought feedback early on as they began work on a project and later on after work was completed. Thus, creative people actively seek feedback from leaders. And as Hemlin and Olsson (2011) found, this feedback is typically proactive, to improve the work, and occurs in regular, ongoing team meetings. Thus, leaders must structure and direct regular team meetings. Indeed, meeting management skills, such as preparing agendas, setting times, and so on (Yukl, 1998), are critical for leading creative efforts.

Leaders in meetings, however, will be asked to appraise the work done. In this regard, a study by Lonergan, Scott, and Mumford (2004) is of some importance. They asked people, some 150 in all, to assume the role of a marketing director. They were asked to review candidate ideas for advertising campaigns developed by teams working for them and prepare a plan for a final campaign – a campaign appraised by judges for a quality and originality. In one manipulation, participants were presented with either high-quality ideas or highly original ideas drawn from earlier work by Redmond, Mumford, and Teach (1993). In the other manipulation, they were encouraged to apply efficiency standards or innovation standards in appraising ideas. It was found that the most creative advertising campaigns were obtained when highly original ideas were appraised with respect to operating efficiency standards, and high-quality ideas were appraised with respect to innovation standards.

One implication of these findings is that leaders, in providing feedback, must compensate for deficiencies in the work done. Of course, to compensate for deficiencies, leaders must have the expertise needed to recognize these deficiencies and be able to criticize the work presented. In keeping with this observation, Gibson and Mumford (2013) asked people to assume the role of the leader of a marketing team criticizing plans for expansion of a clothing line to a new region. Prior to preparing their plans, plans appraised for quality, originality, and elegance, leaders were asked to provide criticisms of these ideas. It was found that the most creative problem solutions were produced by those who provided a limited number of deep, crucial criticisms. Thus, leaders must cut to the bone, the key issues, in providing creative people with feedback.

The other implication of the Lonergan, Scott, and Mumford (2004) study is perhaps more subtle. In evaluating ideas, leaders are themselves actively engaged in the production process seeking to identify and compensate for potential deficiencies. Thus, idea evaluation is not a passive process. Instead, viable idea evaluation on the part of leaders requires substantial creative thinking skills: How do I "fix" this thing? In fact, in a study of leader development, Mumford et al. (2000) found that these creative appraisal skills develop rather slowly due to the need for experience in working in a field. Put more directly, leaders of creative efforts need experience, lots of experience, to effectively evaluate creative work.

People, in evaluating ideas, however, evidence a rather consistent set of biases. Blair and Mumford (2007) presented people with a set of candidate ideas that might be funded by a foundation. Ideas presented were varied with respect to their content. And, it was found that the ideas people funded were not the novel, original ideas. Instead, they were ideas that could be readily implemented, at low cost, serving the needs of many. Thus, leaders, in evaluating, must avoid focusing only on immediate payoffs when appraising the work done by project teams.

In this regard, however, a study by Licuanan, Dailey, and Mumford (2007) is of some importance. They asked people to assume the role of a marketing manager appraising the ideas of six different project teams where the originality of the teams' ideas was varied. Manipulations were induced to encourage active analysis of interactions within the teams and active analysis of idea originality. It was found that active analysis of idea originality and active analysis of interactional processes in the team resulted in leaders accepting more original ideas. Thus, leaders who actively search for originality and are actively involved with their teams on a day-to-day basis are those who are most likely to recognize, and improve, the creative work of their team.

## 4.5 What Do I Do After Evaluation?

The Licuanan, Dailey, and Mumford (2007) study is also of some interest because it points to the importance of leaders actively monitoring the work being done in creative teams. Leader monitoring is a complex activity (Day, Riggio, & Mulligan, 2020). One key aspect of leaders monitoring activities is monitoring both the performance and developmental needs of individuals working on the creative effort (Smither, 2012). Indeed, effective leaders of creative efforts often seek expressly to develop the professional expertise of their workforce by providing access to key collaborations, conferences, and other relevant organizational functions (Hemlin & Olsson, 2011). In the case of creative workers, however, this monitoring should not be so tight that it results in perceptions of overly close supervision. Instead, performance monitoring is typically developmental and task based.

With this said, leaders must also actively monitor the status of the work completed to date and the problems arising in completing this work with leaders seeking to resolve these problems. Although many of these problems are often mundane, not all are. Thus, leaders of creative teams establish monitoring diagnostics and attend to the status of the work with respect to these diagnostics. At times these diagnostics may be quite objective – for example, schedule performance. At other times, these diagnostics may be more subtle – for example, appropriate debate among team members given project issues or unexpected increases in error rates. Regardless of the diagnostics applied, what is clear is that successful leaders of creative efforts identify a set of viable monitoring diagnostics and actively attend to, and appraise, the status of the work, and the people doing the work, with respect to these diagnostics.

In fact, active appraisal of monitoring diagnostics may prove especially important for the leaders of creative efforts because crises often arise as people work on creative projects. Drazin, Glynn, and Kazanjian (1999) conducted a qualitative study of a new product introduction, a new airplane, and found crises emerged, crises of differing levels of significance, throughout the new product development effort. With respect to crises, leaders play four key roles. First, they call attention to the existence and significance of the crisis. Second, they engage in active, crisis-based, sensemaking activities to ensure all team members understand the crisis and how to react to it. Third, they organize crisis response teams, directing these teams with respect to key issues that need to be addressed to resolve the crisis (DeChurch et al., 2011). Fourth, in resolving these crises, creative ideas provided by leaders are often of critical importance (Mumford et al., 2007). The need for leaders to exercise creative thought in helping creative teams address emerging crises, however, implies that leaders of creative efforts need adequate emotional self-regulation.

Often crises pass in creative efforts, and as projects proceed to fielding, one might assume the work of the leader is done. Leaders, however, are typically actively involved in project fielding (Kidder, 1981) – with the leader using experiences in project fielding as a basis for subsequent creative work. Put differently, leaders learn, and actively seek to learn, about what did and did not work in a new product development effort – learning that might serve to initiate another series of creative projects.

Of course, it is not just the leader who learns from creative efforts, it is also members of the project team and the firm as a whole. Thus, leaders of creative efforts should, and sometimes do, take responsibility for disseminating lessons learned from creative efforts throughout the institution. More directly, however, at times projects must be reconfigured due to problems encountered. And, such project reconfigurations will require a new cycle of planning and sensemaking on the part of leaders. Regardless of whether a product has emerged from a creative effort or the project has been reconfigured, leaders must attend to the needs of the individuals working in creative teams.

## 5 Leading the People

Clearly, those asked to lead creative efforts in firms have much to do. They must scan, plan, evaluate, and monitor – activities that require not only expertise but also substantial creative thinking on the part of leaders (Connelly et al., 2000). Our observations with regard to monitoring, however, point to another key activity of those asked to lead creative efforts. Such leaders must lead the people doing the work. Although leaders may structure the work of creative teams, they must exercise influence with respect to the *people* working within this structure (Mumford et al., 2018).

Typically, in discussions of leadership, we assume influence is always exercised through contact, direct contact, between leaders and followers. And how leaders interact with their followers is, in fact, of some importance (Reiter-Palmon & Paulus, 2019). The actions leaders must take to lead the group, however, need not always involve direct interactions or, for that matter, attempts to motivate followers. Indeed, given the high levels of motivation commonly seen in creative people, remember they are achievement motivated, driven, persistent, and domineering; it may be more important for leaders to channel motivation than motivate followers per se.

The need for effective leadership of creative teams, or groups, however, rests on another set of findings. The creative problems that emerge in firms are highly complex. The complexity of these problems is such that virtually always people *must* work with others. Thus, in discussions of creativity and innovation in firms we commonly speak of and structure our thinking, in terms of project teams. On the other hand, groups, or teams, do not encourage creative thinking.

Many studies have compared groups asked to generate ideas while working on divergent thinking tasks to nominal groups or individuals working alone (e.g. Diehl & Stroebe, 1987; Mullen, Johnson, & Salas, 1991; Paulus, 1989; Paulus & Yang, 2000). The finding obtained in these studies point to a straightforward conclusion: people working alone always outperform groups with respect to both the number of ideas produced and the originality of those ideas. Many reasons underlie the ineffectiveness of teams working on creative problems: (1) people loaf and let others do the work, (2) in group settings, process loss is induced by waiting for others, (3) groups induce conformity pressures on members, often pressures limiting the range and originality of the ideas produced, and (4) it takes resources to work with others, resources which limit potential investment in the creative problem.

These problems are noteworthy, in part, because they point to certain strategies for structuring *how* teams should go about working on creative problems (Putman & Paulus, 2009). However, the existence of these problems also underscores the need for effective leadership of creative teams (Paulus, Dzindolet, & Kohn, 2012). For example, leaders, by encouraging participation, may minimize conformity pressures. Leaders, by engaging others in the work to be done, may minimize social loafing. These observations, in turn, however, point to a crucial issue: What must leaders do to lead creative teams?

## 5.1 Who to Recruit?

The first, and one of the most important, issue to be addressed in this regard is who should the leader recruit to work on creative teams. Hunter, Neely, and Gutworth (2018) make the key, basic point in this regard. Given the need for expertise in any creative problem-solving effort, those recruited to join creative teams must have the expertise needed to work on the problem at hand. Thus, leaders need to be able to appraise the bench skills of those they will ask to do creative work. And, they must be able to appraise peoples' creative thinking skills. Put differently, leaders of creative efforts must be good judges of talent, albeit talent with respect to the creative problem at hand.

In this regard, however, two other issues must be borne in mind. Teams, especially creative teams, are doing complex work. Thus, in appraising talent, leaders must recognize they will need an appropriate mix of expertise and thinking skills. In fact, one factor contributing to Oppenheimer's skill as a leader of creative efforts was his ability to appraise the mix of expertise needed for any given project (Bird & Sherwin, 2005). Another issue leaders must take into account is the stage of project development (Mumford, Bedell-Avers, & Hunter, 2008). The mix of expertise needed on project teams will shift as projects move from initial scanning to ultimate fielding. Thus, technical expertise alone may be sufficient in early technical scanning efforts. As projects move to prototyping, however, practical experience and familiarity with the firm, and its processes, will become more important.

In appraising talent, leaders, in a search for assured project success, often try to load as many potential creative contributors into the team as they possibly can. One way this is done is by drawing individuals from as wide a range of backgrounds as possible. People often assume that background diversity will result in more creative teams, in which diversity with respect to gender, ethnicity, and school is held to contribute to creativity. Broadly speaking, however, diversity with respect to background and surface diversity does not contribute to creative performance (Mannix & Neale, 2005; Van Knippenberg & Schippers, 2007). Put differently, in aggregate, superficial diversity has no effect on creativity. Note this is good news, although at times, for example, gender faultlines (Van der Zee et al., 2009) may inhibit team performance while at other times it may encourage creative performance by extending the range of stakeholder contacts (Hirst et al., 2015).

In contrast, functional diversity, diversity in expertise, skills, and with respect to the demands of the project at hand does consistently contribute, positively, to team creative performance (Paulus, Dzindolet, & Kohn, 2012). The impact of functional diversity is that it increases the range of knowledge and skills within creative teams. In fact, functional diversity has been found to be especially beneficial when there is a need for careful processing of information and technical debate under conditions where team members feel a sense of connection with each other and have a sense of psychological safety (Caldwell & O'Reilly, 2003).

Of course, as team size increases, so will diversity, both superficial and functional diversity. However, one must also ask how many people should be recruited for creative teams? And, how many of those recruited should be creative? Fielding of innovative new products is typically positively related to team size (DeRosa, Smith, & Hantula, 2007) – although such effects reflect necessary firm-level investments in product development and fielding. In initial idea development, however, smaller group size appears to contribute to creativity (Mullen, Johnson, & Salas, 1991). These observations, of course, suggest that the number of individuals recruited should be consistent with the stage of product development where teams should be no larger, or smaller, than they need to be.

With regard to the number of creative people recruited, however, a somewhat different concern emerges. Miron-Spektor, Erez, and Naveh (2011) studied forty-one research and development teams. They found that teams producing radical innovations were composed of some highly creative people but also some less creative but more conscientious and pragmatic people. Thus, not all people assigned to innovative teams should be highly creative. Instead, creative people must have support, support that ensures the details of the work are attended to, and support that acts to moderate the conflict likely to emerge among creative people.

People in general, and creative people specifically, cannot just be ordered to take on a creative project. And, recruitment of key team members is typically the responsibility of the leader (Kidder, 1981). To recruit creative people, however, leaders must sell the project and sell the project to the person. Earlier we noted that creative people are professionally focused and invested in professional achievement and advancement of their professional careers. Accordingly, it is clear how leaders of creative efforts should sell a project to creative people. They should describe how the project, if successful, would contribute to their professional reputation and how work on the project would serve to advance their careers both professionally and within the firm. What should be recognized here, however, is for leaders to do these sales they must know where to look – what schools produce the kind of people I am looking for? In which other firms are people who are likely to be invested in the project currently working? Where do people with such interests currently reside in the firm? What is of note here, however, is that to answer such questions leaders of creative efforts need not only a depth of understanding of the project, they must also know the profession and the firm, as well as possess a real understanding of the interests and ambitions of those they are recruiting to work on a creative project.

## 5.2 How Should They Work Together?

Recruiting people to work in creative teams is essential. By the same token those who are recruited must work together on the project. And, bearing in mind the autonomy, domineering, and critical nature of creative people, it is not at all clear that they will work together on a project. Thus, leaders must act to establish conditions that will encourage creative people to work together as a team. In this regard, it is important to recognize that by formulating project plans and articulating a clear mission, a mission framed with respect to certain key constraints, leaders provide a framework within which team performance becomes possible.

Articulation of this plan, of course, results in the leader providing a vision for the team. Hülsheger, Anderson, and Salgado (2009) conducted a meta-analysis examining the effects of team level variables on innovative achievement. They found that the vision for project work, a vision articulated by team leaders, was, in fact, a powerful influence on subsequent creative achievement. In this regard, however, it is important to recognize that it is not enough for leaders of creative teams simply to state their vision in broad terms. They must also engage in extensive sensegiving activities. In other words, they must describe, and ensure team members understand, how the work is to unfold with respect to key goals, work activities needed to attain these goals, and constraints of these work activities.

Leaders' sensegiving activities are noteworthy because they establish shared goals among members of a project team. Gilson and Shalley (2004) contrasted more and less effective teams with respect to their engagement in creative work processes, and, they found, more creative teams were characterized by shared goals. What is of note in this regard, however, is that it is not enough simply for team members to have shared goals; leaders' sensegiving activities must also delineate interdependence among various subgoals associated with overarching goals and describe how various team members accountable for these subgoals depend on each other. In keeping with this observation, Hülsheger, Anderson, and Salgado (2009) found that perceived goal interdependence among team members contributes to creativity and innovation.

Goal interdependencies, and leader sensegiving intended to help team members understand these interdependencies, are noteworthy for another reason. Such known interdependencies encourage internal communication with creative teams. In a meta-analytic study, Damanpour (1991) found that internal communication within teams is positively related to creativity and innovation. Indeed, at least part of the reason leaders of creative groups conduct regular team meetings is to encourage such internal communication. Internal communication in creative teams, however, occurs not only in team meetings but also over the course of day-to-day activities. And, leaders can, and do, take actions to encourage day-to-day communication. They may simply tell two or three people in the meeting to talk to each other about a certain issue. Alternatively, they may encourage team members to share early findings on task-based listservs. Although internal communication is needed, the issue here is not the simple amount of communication (Kratzer, Leenders, & Van Engelen, 2004) but rather deep, collaborative communication. Thus, leaders should take actions to encourage task-relevant communication while minimizing talking just for the sake of talking – perhaps by asking technical questions or actively raising technical concerns in online discussion groups.

It is not just internal communication that counts for creative teams, it is also external communication. Studies by Anacona and Caldwell (1992), Howell and Shea (2006), and Keller (2001) all indicate that the intensity of external communication contributes to innovation. External communication provides requisite information with regard to the creative work while encouraging ongoing learning. It may also help to build support for, and learning about, the creative efforts across the firm. What should be recognized here, however, is that it is often leaders of creative teams who arrange for such external contacts. And, it is often the leaders of creative teams who point out the need for these external contacts.

More broadly, leaders of creative teams must encourage ongoing learning among team members with respect to the problem at hand. One way leaders encourage ongoing learning is by encouraging team members to reflect on the reasons for success, or failure, in past work – team reflexivity. In one study along these lines, Carter and West (1998) studied BBC production teams. They found that team reflexivity was positively related to both team performance and production of innovative products. Tjosvold, Tang, and West (2004), in a study of Chinese teams, found that team reflexivity was not only positively related to innovation but was also higher when team members were working with respect to a shared set of key goals. Thus, leaders' mission definition and sensegiving may lay a foundation for team reflexivity and team learning.

The need for team reflexivity and team learning in creative projects, however, points to another issue of some importance. All members of the team must participate in this learning exercise. Thus, Zhou, Hirst, and Shipton (2012) found participation to be positively related to creativity, especially when team members were intellectually engaged in the task at hand. These findings are by no means unique. Mumford et al. (2002) stressed the importance of active participation by all team members in creative projects. What they note, however, is that leaders are often a key mechanism encouraging active participation. For example, leaders may ask why someone has been quiet during a meeting to encourage them to share their ideas. Similarly, when an approach for addressing a project issue has been proposed, leaders might ask other team members to indicate what they see as the strengths and weaknesses of this approach.

Clearly, there are a number of ways those asked to lead creative efforts can encourage participation. Bearing in mind the critical, domineering nature of creative people, however, participation can be expected to induce conflict among team members. Conflict, of course, comes in many forms – it might be personal or technical. Broadly speaking, personalized conflicts always decrease the performance of creative teams due to their negative impact on collaboration. In contrast, Chen (2006) found that technical conflict, but not personalized conflict, contributes to creativity among R&D teams. In this regard, however, it is important to bear in mind two caveats. First, Kratzer, Leenders, and Van Engelen (2006) found that technical conflict was more beneficial early as opposed to late in project development cycles. Second, technical conflict is only beneficial up to a point (De Dreu, 2006) – in part because technical conflict can spill over into personal conflict. This observation is noteworthy because it suggests that those leading creative efforts must actively manage conflicts. Accordingly, leaders must allow only technical conflict and discount, and often actively criticize personal conflict as harmful to team performance. Leaders, moreover, must use techniques, such as integration or accommodation, to encourage constructive technical conflict (Song, Dyer, & Thieme, 2006).

With regard to technical conflict, and participation, however, another point must be borne in mind. People are likely to participate and advance their ideas, including ideas in conflict with others, only when they feel safe to do so. This point is important because it implies that people must feel psychologically safe to engage in creative work. And, in fact, studies by Amabile and Kramer (2011a) and Carmeli, Gelbard, and Reiter-Palmon (2013) have indicated that feelings of psychological safety are critical to encouraging people to express their ideas and engage in creative work. In firms, however, the actions taken by leaders are a key force shaping peoples' feelings of psychological safety (Amabile et al., 2004). Thus, leaders should not punish followers for failure. Leaders should couch criticisms by noting what was done "well" as well as what was done "wrong." Leaders should recognize the time and effort people have devoted to executing both creative tasks *and* tasks supporting others creative work. These, and a host of other actions by leaders, all serve to induce feelings of psychological safety in teams – feelings of safety needed to undertake creative work.

Leaders, however, do not just establish feelings of safety with regard to pursuing creative work, they shape how people perceive their work environment (James, James, & Ashe, 1990). Over the years many studies have examined how perceptions of the work environment influence creativity and innovative achievement. In a meta-analysis of these studies, Hunter, Bedell, and Mumford (2007) found that perceptions of the work environment were strongly positively related to creativity and innovative achievement producing a Cohen's $\Delta$ of .75. Moreover, three dimensions of climate were found to be especially powerful predictors of creativity and innovative achievement: (1) positive interpersonal exchange ($\Delta = .91$), (2) intellectual stimulation ($\Delta = .85$), and (3) professional challenge ($\Delta = .85$).

In a subsequent study of some 399 research and development personnel, Hunter et al. (2019) sought to identify the key variables contributing to perceptions of creative climate. Using confirmatory factor analytic techniques, they identified five key dimensions of creative climate: (1) autonomy and stimulation, (2) positive peer exchange, (3) leader direction and encouragement, (4) organizational resources and support, and (5) organizational integration and extension. Leaders, as will be apparent in our discussion of leading the firm, can take action to ensure organizational support and organizational integration. With respect to leading creative teams, however, intellectual stimulation, positive peer exchange, and leader direction and encouragement appear to be the critical aspects of the environment for creative work that leaders have control over.

With regard to direction and encouragement, clearly leaders' plans, their definition of the mission, and their sensegiving activities are all of some importance to peoples' perceptions of their work environment. As important as these directive activities are, however, one cannot forget an old adage – if you don't ask for it, you won't get it. And, in fact, Rietzschel, Nijstad, and Stroebe (2014) have found that when people work on creative problem-solving tasks, instructions to be creative contribute to idea generation and production of more original solutions. Accordingly, leaders should both designate critical areas of project work where creative thinking is required and ask the team to produce something creative! Support, however, is not simply a matter of requesting creative work, leaders must also expressly recognize the value of the creative work undertaken. Sometimes appreciative actions are quite straightforward – congratulate people, congratulate them in front of the team, for creative accomplishments such as publications or patents. At other times, appreciative actions may be more subtle – for example, acknowledging, often publicly, extra effort put in on a creative problem or asking those involved to describe their work to the team or other key units in the firm.

It may be more difficult to see how leaders can ensure positive peer exchange – after all, it is peer exchange. Leaders, however, can take a number of actions to encourage positive peer exchange. For example, team social events might be encouraged by the leader as one technique to build supportive relationships. Leaders might encourage younger and older team members to work together both to develop younger workers and to build a sense of team collaboration. Leaders might encourage subteam competition, assuming subteam membership is needed, as yet another way to encourage positive peer exchange. Leaders might expressly note their approval in meetings for team members who have helped someone else complete an important piece of work. Clearly, this is not an exhaustive list of actions leaders might take to encourage positive peer exchange. What should be noted here, however, is that a variety of actions might be taken by leaders to encourage perceptions of positive peer exchange.

Intellectual stimulation and work on professionally challenging tasks, work where the individual is granted sufficient autonomy, are the final key climate dimensions. And, in fact, intellectual stimulation and challenge are, in part, determined by the leader as they formulate project plans and articulate the mission of the team. Indeed, when sensegiving, providing team members with an understanding of the professional significance of the project, and its potential impact on the firm, is one way leaders can challenge followers. Such efforts, however, can be more subtle – for example, noting how the work advances prior efforts or noting how a project might reshape the business done in the firm.

However, it is not just through planning and mission definition that leaders establish an intellectually stimulating environment (Boies, Fiset, & Gill, 2015). The questions leaders ask about work, especially deep, insightful questions, will help establish an intellectually stimulating environment. Asking team members to pursue interesting "leads" arising in their work often proves intellectually stimulating. Encouraging team members to communicate with professionals outside the work group about the nature and significance of their work is not only motivating – creative people also find it intellectually stimulating. These and other behaviors intended to encourage follower intellectual engagement appear especially important in establishing a climate for creativity given the various findings emerging in studies of transformational leadership and creativity – all of which indicate leader intellectual stimulation; stimulation that, in part, depends on the leader's expertise and creative thinking skills is the key, critical variable contributing to follower creativity (Boies, Fiset, & Gill, 2015; Eisenbeiss & Boerner, 2013; Jaussi & Dionne, 2003; Sosik, Kahai, & Avolio, 1998).

## 5.3 How Should You Interact with Followers?

The findings with regard to leader member exchange and their impact on creativity and innovation (e.g. Tierney, Farmer, & Graen, 1999) point to another issue of concern to those asked to lead creative teams – how should the leader interact with followers? How one interacts with followers, of course, depends on their personality. And, the personality of creative people is distinct. As noted earlier, they are critical, domineering, and autonomous. These personality characteristics are noteworthy because creative people are unlikely to automatically trust the leader, even though studies by Cheung and Wong (2011) and Lee (2015) indicate that trust in the leader is positively related to creativity.

Trust is seen as the willingness to ascribe good intentions to, and have confidence in, the words and actions of others. A variety of influences lead people to trust others, including perceptions of competence, sincerity, or authenticity, and behavioral consistency or keeping one's word (Schoorman, Mayer, & Davis, 2007). For those asked to lead creative efforts, these observations have an important implication. Leaders must keep their word and, to the extent others perceive the leader as keeping their word, commitment to the creative project and satisfaction with the work will increase. In this regard, however, in a population of critical, autonomous people, violations of trust may prove particularly difficult to repair with potentially disastrous implications for the work.

In firms, trust is often built upon peoples' perceptions of justice. Justice is not a general construct but is commonly construed as involving three distinct attributes: (1) distributive justice, (2) procedural justice, and (3) organizational justice (Cohen-Charash & Spector, 2001). Clearly, institutions grant leaders some control over when and what rewards, distributive justice, are provided for the work of followers. What should be clear here is that leaders' allocation of rewards must be fair with rewards being provided based on the individual's contributions to the work. These rewards, among creative people, need not always be monetary. Indeed, increased professional visibility or access to key rotational assignments may be as powerful an influence on creative people as monetary reward. Regardless of reward type, however, fair, equitable distribution of rewards will prove crucial in building perceptions of justice.

Creative people, however, are typically professional, and professionals have a unique concern with procedures (Bennich-Björkman, 2017). Leaders, accordingly, must define to their followers the procedures that will be used in decision making – who makes the decision, the leader or the team, what information will be required to make a decision, under what conditions is a constraint considered satisfied, and so on. The key point here, however, is that once defined, leaders must follow procedures consistently, although these procedures cannot be so tightly defined as to undermine flexibility and should be structured to stress the need for procedural openness. Although organizational justice may seem beyond the scope of a team leader, how leaders communicate organizational decisions, and help followers make sense of organizational decisions, will have a noteworthy impact on followers' perceptions of organizational justice – especially when the leader actively, publicly represents the concerns of followers to the organization.

Followers' perceptions of trust and justice in the leader are important for another reason. Earlier we noted that a key role of leaders of creative efforts is providing followers with feedback concerning their work – feedback which serves to compensate for deficiencies in the work (Lonergan, Scott, & Mumford, 2004). As a result, leaders' interactions with their followers will depend on their demonstrated expertise and viable creative problem-solving skills. In fact, expertise seems to be the critical variable shaping the willingness of creative people to accept, and act on, influence attempts by the leader. Indeed, leaders of creative efforts seem to be aware of the importance of exhibiting professional expertise and creative thinking skills. What should be recognized here, however, is that it is not the perception or manipulation of expertise perceptions that counts to creative people but rather demonstration of expertise, and creative thinking skills, in the appraisal of follower work. If followers do not "see" expertise and creative thinking in their leaders, leader criticisms of their work may be viewed as little more than an insult.

The need for leaders' demonstration of expertise in their interactions with followers is noteworthy for another reason. Leaders serve as role models and, in the case of creative professionals, role models of professional success. One implication of this statement is that leaders in interacting with followers must model professional conduct. Not only should leaders model professional conduct, however, a key role played by leaders is providing followers with access to professional networks and expertise lying outside their current scope. Indeed, professional access provided by leaders has been found to be a powerful motivating force for creative people (Styhre & Gluch, 2009).

Another implication of the foregoing observation, however, pertains to mentoring. Leaders in interacting with followers and providing critical feedback with respect to their work are also engaged in teaching. And, creative people, although autonomous, seek out mentors or teachers (Mumford et al., 2005) with mentoring proving a critical influence on acquisition of expertise and creative thinking skills. Thus, the leaders of creative efforts must be as much teachers as managers. This point is important for two reasons. Leaders of creative efforts must know their people and their capabilities, scaffolding work assignments in such a way as to encourage the acquisition of new expertise based on the needs and goals of that particular follower. Not only must leaders seek to teach followers, instruction often prized by creative people, they must also express confidence in the followers' ability to handle work assignments and handle work assignments creatively. Put differently, leaders in interacting with followers must build a sense of creative self-efficacy (Tierney & Farmer, 2002).

The need for leaders of creative efforts to teach, and teach in such a way as to build a sense of creative self-efficacy, points to a final issue concerning how leaders should interact with followers. Leaders of creative efforts do not just serve the work and serve the firm – they also serve followers. This point is underscored by studies examining the impact of servant leadership on creativity and innovation. For example, Yoshida et al. (2014) appraised the creative performance of teams while assessing servant leadership behaviors, such as calling, awareness, foresight, growth, community building and stewardship (Barbuto & Wheeler, 2006), finding that servant leadership was positively related to team creative performance. In another study along these lines, Jaiswal and Dhar (2017) assessed the impact of servant leadership behavior on the creative performance of forty-eight teams. They found not only that servant leadership was positively related to team creativity but also that servant leadership behaviors resulted in greater follower trust and thriving. These findings are noteworthy because they suggest that leaders of creative efforts must build a sense of community in their teams. Indeed, the sense of community, "we happy few," may provide followers with the resilience needed to tolerate the substantial, ongoing threat of failure that characterizes all creative work.

The idea that leaders of creative efforts act as servants and teachers, building a sense of local community, has another, albeit often overlooked, implication. Leaders of creative efforts must represent this community. One aspect of this representation function is representing the work of their followers, and the unique capabilities of their followers, to the professional community. And, although strong evidence bearing on this point is lacking, there is reason to suspect that, given their professional focus, creative people will find leaders' representation of them and their work of substantial value. Leaders, however, must represent followers, and the team as a whole, not just to the profession. They must also represent followers and the team to the institution in which they are working. And, leaders' representation of creative individuals, and creative teams, to the institution as a whole constitutes the third major theme evident in the work of those asked to lead creative efforts.

## 6 Leading the Firm

In firms, leaders serve in a boundary role (Katz & Kahn, 1978). The term boundary role refers to the expectation that individuals within this role will establish contact with, and exchange information and services, other institutional units. Although our stereotype of creative leaders is that they live in a dark closet set far, far away from the "real" institution, those asked to lead creative efforts are not locked away but instead serve in a critical boundary role. Indeed, as noted earlier, boundary role activities on the part of those asked to lead creative efforts are evident in the need for leaders to represent the team to both the profession and the organization in which the team is working.

For those asked to lead creative efforts, however, the boundary role activities involved in their work go well beyond simply representing the team. As noted earlier, leaders of creative efforts must maintain contact with, and active involvement in, their professional field to facilitate acquisition and dissemination of technical information and ensure recruitment of requisite expertise for project teams (Hülsheger, Anderson, & Salgado, 2009). Leaders' representational activities as occupants of a key boundary role, however, are not limited to the profession. Leaders of creative efforts must represent the work to the firm as a whole and to key constituencies within the firm. Not only must they represent the work, and the team, to the institution, they must also represent the concerns of the firm, and other key units in the firm, to the project team. And, without these representational, boundary spanning activities, creative work and the fielding of viable new products is unlikely to occur.

### 6.1 How Do I Get Resources?

In firms, both for-profit and not-for-profit institutions, resources are closely guarded and under the control of top management (Schult & Wolff, 2012). The control top management teams' exercise over resources arises from three considerations. First, capital must be conserved for critical institutional activities involved in product production and day-to-day goods and services. Second, resources must be invested to ensure attainment of the firm's strategic objectives. Third, in firms, multiple units make multiple demands for available resources, both financial and social. As a result, there is never enough to go around, and top management teams must make decisions about when and where to invest scarce resources (Cao, Simsek, & Zhang, 2010).

Creative work, however, is a costly undertaking. Part of the cost of creative work is direct – for example, salaries for team members. Part of the cost of creative work is indirect – disruption of organizational production processes, costs associated with entry into new markets, new staffing demands, and new learning requirements in multiple units in the firm. Given the substantial direct and indirect costs associated with creative work (Chandy & Tellis, 1998, 2000), it seems clear that top management support for creative work in firms is critical (Daellenbach, McCarthy, & Schoenecker, 1999; Hegarty & Hoffman, 1990).

This point is underscored in a study by Dougherty and Hardy (1996b). They conducted interviews with some 150 innovators working in 15 large firms. Interviews focused on resource acquisition and integration of the innovative efforts with other firm activities. More and less successful innovative efforts were contrasted; it was found that solving resource problems, acquiring requisite resources, and linking the creative work to firm strategy were critical to project success. Other work has shown that the support evidenced by top management must be sustained and made visible to the firm as a whole – with top management teams providing both fiscal and social support (Chen et al., 2016).

So how do leaders of creative teams obtain the support and commitment of top management to creative projects? It appears leaders must champion their creative work to top management (Markham, 2000; Markham & Aiman-Smith, 2001). Studies of those championing creative work in firms indicate champions recognize the value of the project to the firm. They advocate for the project to top management often exploiting personal networks to gain access to top management and build support for projects (Howell & Higgins, 1990). Moreover, as Markham and Smith (2017) point out, champions are not only knowledgeable about the creative effort but are also willing to educate others with respect to its potential significance. Thus, leaders, when working as champions, must understand the project and its implications for the firm using personal connections, often connections to top management, to advocate for the project.

Although the need for leaders to champion creative projects to top management is clear, the question remains as to how champions are successful in "selling" creative efforts to top management. The issue has been addressed in a study by Howell and Boies (2004). They obtained nineteen matched pairs of champions and nonchampions involved in various new product development efforts. Interviews with these champions and nonchampions were conducted. Content analysis of these interviews indicated champions, as opposed to

nonchampions, were more enthusiastic about the creative project and its implications for the firm and were willing to use informal connections to sell the
project. Again, a finding indicating leaders of creative efforts need contacts and
contacts to the top management team.

More centrally, champions were found to also promote ideas through formal
reporting channels in the firm. The success of formal idea promotion, however,
was found to depend on contextual knowledge of the firm. Put differently,
champions sold creative work with respect to the value of the work for firm
strategy, market share, and growth potential. Thus, the leaders of creative efforts
must not only have expertise with respect to the profession, they must also have
expertise with respect to the firm and be able to envision the implications of the
work, if successful, for the firm in the future.

The other key variable that emerged in the Howell and Boies (2004) study
is that champions, as opposed to nonchampions, were more effective in
packaging creative work for top management. In other words, they needed
to know how to describe the content and implications of the work in terms
that members of the top management team could understand. This finding is
noteworthy, in part, because it implies that the leaders of creative efforts must
be able to speak to, and teach, people from other backgrounds about the
nature and significance of a creative project. This instruction, however, is not
the dry instruction of the classroom. They must engage, and excite, the top
management team with respect to the significance and implications of the
work. In other words, the leaders of creative efforts must sell the work, and
sell it to senior executives as people, as to how it might play out in the future
for the firm.

One implication of this observation is that leaders of creative efforts must be
flexible. On the one hand, they must know the work and the profession, and, on
the other hand, they must know the work and the firm. Perhaps more centrally,
however, they must be able to integrate the work being done with respect to its
implications for the firm. The other noteworthy implication of this observation,
however, is that the leaders of creative efforts cannot be isolated from the firm.
Instead, they must understand, and be actively involved, in shaping the strategy
of the firm vis-à-vis the creative work being done.

Although championing may result in a firm devoting resources to a creative
effort, it must be recognized that both firms and creative projects change over
time along with the resources needed to support the effort (Mumford, Bedell-
Avers, & Hunter, 2008). This observation is noteworthy because it implies that
championing will be an ongoing activity on the part of those asked to lead
creative efforts. As projects proceed to prototyping and fielding, new, additional
"sales" to top management will be needed. Moreover, the "sales" will move

from highly prospective to directly tangible as projects develop (O'Connor, 1998).

These observations are noteworthy for another reason: The investment required from top management will change as projects move from initial exploratory scanning to prototyping and fielding, with "sales" occurring at each stage. And, a related question must be asked at each stage, and in each stage: How much support, tangible fiscal support, should be requested? Although people, in general, want to ask for everything, the available evidence indicates that asking for just enough for the time being is the most appropriate approach for "selling" creative projects. On the one hand, creative teams need institutional resources, staff, equipment, and so on (Hunter et al., 2019). On the other hand, too much slack resource appears to inhibit creative work (Nohria & Gulati, 1996).

Although it is critical for the leaders of creative efforts to obtain the physical and fiscal resources needed to do the work, leaders championing efforts play another key role. Creative work is not always seen by members of a firm as either legitimate or desirable (Bergek, Jacobsson, & Sandén, 2008; Sturdy et al., 2009). Top management support for a project, however, provides a mechanism that serves to legitimate the creative effort. Thus, if top management, the embodiment of what is legitimate in a firm (Hambrick, 2015), actively articulates the value of a creative effort, acceptance of, and support for, the creative effort throughout the firm will increase. Thus, those asked to lead creative efforts are not simply seeking fiscal resources, they are also seeking social support from top management for the creative effort.

The available evidence indicates that top management's articulation of support for a creative effort should be ongoing (Dougherty & Hardy, 1996b). Thus, if top management *appears* to drop support for a project, so will the rest of the firm. Thus, leaders of creative efforts must actively ensure *ongoing* support of top management throughout the course of a project – recognizing that the nature and intensity of legitimation activities may change over time. Accordingly, leaders of creative efforts can be expected to engage in ongoing monitoring of top management's legitimation efforts providing top management with feedback concerning the nature and success of such efforts.

The support top management provided for creative efforts, however, is noteworthy in another way. Support from top management for a creative effort not only legitimates the creative effort, it also opens the doors of other units. The development and fielding of new products and processes typically involves multiple organizational units – from purchasing to marketing to finance (Hadjikosta & Friedrich, 2020). And, active top management support for the creative effort encourages other units, units less directly involved in the creative effort, to provide the support needed.

## 6.2 How Do I Get Unit Support?

The support of units of the firm, beyond top management, is necessary for both "positive" and "negative" reasons. Turning first to "negative" reasons: key units in a firm, if they reject a creative effort, may effectively kill the effort. And, in fact, there are many reasons other functional units in a firm may not support a creative effort. The creative effort may disrupt normative business processes, resulting in a loss of efficiency for the unit. The creative effort may entail new business processes and the need for work force skills which the unit finds too costly. The unit may simply not see, or understand, the value of the creative effort for the firm.

The impact of unit rejection on the success of creative efforts is nicely illustrated in a qualitative study by Jelinek and Schoonhoven (1990). They conducted a qualitative study of a shipping firm introducing a new tracking system for shipping containers based on insertion of specialized chips in containers. Not only did the chips and the associated information technology system work, and work well, the effort had the full support of top management. Nonetheless, at least at this time the effort failed, and it failed because the warehouse unit was unwilling to support introduction of the new technology – in part due to unfamiliarity with information technology systems, and, in part, due to changes in requisite work procedures and processes.

On the positive side, there are a variety of reasons why various organizational units might support a creative effort. Some units, for example, marketing and sales, may see a creative effort as opening up new markets and expanding the firm's customer base (e.g. Song & Thieme, 2006). Purchasing may see a creative effort as a vehicle for obtaining new market intelligence about potential suppliers (e.g. McGonagle & Vella, 2012). If innovative new products prove attractive to investors, it often proves easier for firms to acquire the financing needed to support the firm as a whole (e.g. Bronzini & Piselli, 2016). Thus, institutional units have reasons for investing in, as well as rejecting, creative efforts and the innovations flowing from them.

The existence of both potential negative and potential positive reactions to creative efforts poses a challenge for leaders. Leaders of creative efforts must take actions that will minimize negative reactions on the part of other institutional units and maximize positive reactions. So how do leaders garner the support of other relevant organizational units? To begin, leaders must know, and understand, the organizational unit. In fact, leaders of creative efforts may need a rather deep understanding of operations occurring in these units. Not only will leaders need to know what the unit does, they will also need to know the business processes and norms of the unit. In addition, they will also need to know what the key problems are confronting this unit in conducting its business and the skills members of this unit have and do not have. Although it takes time to acquire such knowledge, and knowledge acquisition may require active information gathering on the part of the leader, such knowledge provides a basis for acquiring support from key organizational units.

Again, in acquiring support from other institutional units some degree of championing is required. Assuming, however, that top management is providing support for the creative effort, the intensity of "sales" efforts will decrease. Instead, sales will focus primarily on describing the risks and benefits top management sees with respect to the project at hand.

In obtaining support from other institutional units, the critical concern of the unit will be tied to the potential impact of the creative effort with respect to unit operations (Mumford et al., 2019). As a result, the leader of the creative effort must have some general idea of how the creative effort will impact unit operations – a point already noted. By the same token the leader of the creative effort will not have the same understanding of unit operations as those working in the unit. This observation implies leaders must listen to unit members' concerns, having the listening skills and openness needed to learn from the comments of supporting unit members (Bonet, 2001). Indeed, at times, the issues and concerns broached by supporting units may be of sufficient importance to result in noteworthy changes in the leaders' plans and/or the initiation of new creative efforts.

By the same token, however, members of supporting units will not have the same level of understanding of the creative project as those leading the creative effort. This point is noteworthy because leaders must help the members of support units understand the nature and implications of the creative project. In this regard, the leader is acting as a teacher helping other organizational units make sense of the creative effort and make sense of the creative effort with respect to requisite changes in unit operations (Spreitzer & Sonenshein, 2004).

Although leader sensegiving is needed to build support for a creative effort, for many creative efforts more than sensemaking will be required. Supporting units will need to learn about the implications of the creative effort for unit operations. Indeed, at times this may require the unit to initiate trial programs or initiate its own creative efforts. Under these conditions the leader will be serving as a stimulus for institutional learning. In fact, at times, leaders may need to rotate staff working on the creative effort to support the learning activities of the unit. Thus, leaders must be able to assess the learning needs of key support units and provide these units with resources, staff, briefings, and trial findings needed to support unit learning (Goh & Richards, 1997; McGill, Slocum, & Lei, 1992; Senge, 1995).

Vera and Crossan (2004) have argued that organizational learning requires both exploration and exploitation by units. One implication of this observation is that those asked to lead creative efforts must not only monitor and provide feedback to the team working on the creative project, they must also monitor and provide feedback to key support units. Put somewhat differently, leaders of creative efforts must be willing to serve as consultants to key institutional units needed to support a creative effort.

In this regard, the findings of Chang and Lee (2007) and Noruzy et al. (2013) are of some note. They indicate that a key role played by leaders in organizational learning is transformational. The impact of transformational leadership behavior on organizational learning, however, is largely a function of intellectually stimulating behavior on the part of the leader. Thus, as leaders of creative efforts serve as consultants to supporting units, and as they sell the creative project to supporting units, they must stimulate creative thinking in these units. They must engage the unit in the project, get the unit to ask the right questions, and get the unit to think about new ways of doing things, thus presenting a vision for the project that both involves unit members and enhances the supporting unit in the future.

## 6.3 Can You Get What You Need?

The need for leaders of creative efforts to gather support from other units in a firm is noteworthy for another reason. As projects proceed from scanning and exploration to prototyping and fielding, more expertise, and expertise from different functional units, is required (Mumford, Bedell-Avers, & Hunter, 2008). In other words, leaders must not only build a creative team, they must build and manage cross-functional teams (Jassawalla & Sashittal, 1999; Sethi, Smith, & Park, 2001).

The need for cross-functional teams is nicely illustrated in a meta-analytic study by Troy, Hirunyawipada, and Paswan (2008) of the impact of cross-functional teams on successful new product introductions. They found that effective cross-functional teaming was correlated in the low .20s with the successful introduction of new products. In another study along these lines, Cooper and Kleinschmidt (1995) found that cross-functional teaming was related to successful new product introductions, technical success, and increased profitability across 135 North American and European firms. In still another study along these lines, Valle and Avella (2003) found not only that cross-functional teams contributed to successful new product introductions but also that the processes underlying new product development efforts improved in cross-functional teams.

From the perspective of the leader of a creative effort, however, two crucial questions arise. Who do I recruit from other units as projects move into a cross-functional phase? And, when do I bring these people aboard? To recruit cross-functional team members, especially high-quality cross-functional team members, it is clear the leaders of creative efforts must have accrued top management support and have garnered support from the relevant supporting unit. Indeed, if the supporting unit is not invested in the project, it is unlikely they will make their best people available. Along related lines, leaders in interacting with key support units are also acquiring knowledge regarding the capabilities of members of the support unit and are taking actions likely to bring these individuals into the creative project.

With regard to timing, however, it is not desirable to bring cross-functional expertise into play prior to it being needed for successful product development. The reason for making this statement lies, in part, in team process – different professions have different languages and different goals. And, as a result, incorporation of cross-functional expertise will typically disrupt short-term team performance (Majchrzak, More, & Faraj, 2012). Moreover, inclusion of extraneous knowledge, extraneous at least at that point in the project, will disrupt creative thinking within the project team.

The costs associated with introduction of cross-functional expertise is noteworthy because it implies that leaders must prepare cross-functional imports to join the creative team. Thus, leaders must familiarize the "imports" with both the nature of the project and their expected contribution to the effort. In addition, roles and role expectations should be clearly defined. Accordingly, McDonough (2000) and Norrgren and Schaller (1999) have argued that effective leadership behavior, both consideration and structuring behavior, is critical to importation of expertise into cross-functional teams. These observations, of course, suggest that leaders of creative efforts must both attend to and understand the nature of the people they are bringing aboard to support a project.

Leaders' concerns, however, cannot just be focused on those being brought aboard. At a minimum, leaders must explain to current members of the team why the expertise is being "imported" and how the people being brought in can be expected to contribute to project success. Put somewhat differently, leaders of creative efforts must help team members make sense of the cross-functional teaming requirements. Moreover, as one brings in people with different forms of professional expertise, it becomes more difficult for leaders to rely on professional norms as a crutch for managing the team. This point is important because it implies that leaders of creative efforts may need to attend more to team process and structure in the later phases of a project than in the earlier phases. To complicate matters further, however, those leading creative efforts must still seek to establish an intellectually stimulating, creative work climate, albeit one that is engaging to people from a wider range of backgrounds.

When one considers our foregoing observations, it should be clear those asked to lead creative efforts do not, and cannot, live in isolation. They must champion the creative effort to top management and ensure active support of top management for the creative effort. They must build support for the creative effort among key functional units, not only building support but also encouraging organizational learning with respect to the nature and implications of the creative effort. And, they must import expertise and knowledge from those units, constantly restructuring the project and project team in such a way that multiple forms of expertise can be employed in development of a creative idea into a viable new product or service. Put perhaps most succinctly, leaders must lead the firm, educating the firm, its units, and the people about the nature of the project and its implications.

## 7 Conclusions, Directions, and Needs

Our foregoing observations point to a noteworthy, albeit critical, conclusion. The leadership of creative efforts is among the most, if not the most, complicated forms of leadership we see in firms. Consider just some of what leaders must do. They must be able to plan highly complex work and provide their people with critical, and creative, feedback. They must be able to sell the firm as to the significance of the work even as they look five, ten, or fifteen years downstream. They must be able to explain the work to others, others who lack their professional expertise, taking into account the work being done by those working in other units. They need to know not only the creative work being done but the work done in key functional units as well. They must recruit people, team members, and get a group of people to work together – people who are not inclined to work with others. And, they must establish an intellectually challenging environment where the members of the team trust them and see them as a fair, just person. And, all of this must be done as they lead multiple projects and maintain an active professional career.

Few other jobs evidence similar complexity (Peterson et al., 1999). In fact, a rather compelling argument can be made that it is more difficult to lead creative efforts in a firm than it is to run the firm as a whole (Mumford & Mulhearn, 2019). These observations are noteworthy because they point to both the challenges the leaders of creative efforts face and the challenges confronting firms as they seek to build a cadre of people capable of leading creative efforts.

## 7.1 Questions and Models

The complexity of leading creative efforts presents those asked to lead creative efforts with a number of questions: questions about the nature of creative people, who to recruit, how to provide feedback, and how to obtain requisite resources. And, recognition of this point is the reason we organized this Element with respect to these key questions. These questions, however, and their generality, point to a more basic issue – they all arise from the work leaders of creative efforts are asked to do.

Robledo, Peterson, and Mumford (2012) and Vessey et al. (2014) proposed a model describing the key functions, or work activities, that must be executed by those ask to lead creative efforts. Although this model describes a number of functional activities, it stresses three basic activities that must be executed by those asked to lead creative efforts in firms: lead the work, lead the team, and lead the firm. And, they must be doing all these things simultaneously.

One key point in this regard is that the concerns/issues involved in a creative effort for any one constituency are not guaranteed to be aligned with those of another constituency. What the people doing the work want, typically professional advancement, may not be what the firm wants, perhaps a small incremental improvement on a current product. What the work needs may not be what either the team or the firm wants. These observations are noteworthy because they indicate that those asked to lead creative efforts must not only understand the needs/concerns of these three constituencies, they must also be able to integrate the work, the firm, and the people in such a way as to establish and execute projects of value to all.

The needs for leaders to synthesize, or integrate, these distinct sets of concerns is further complicated by yet another issue. Creative efforts in firms are not just one project. Instead, they are a package of projects, with projects unfolding and changing as they move from initial exploration to prototyping and fielding (Mumford, Bedell-Avers, & Hunter, 2008). Thus, the leadership of creative efforts is an inherently dynamic activity. Although we lack research on how leaders manage this dynamism, this dynamism and the multiple functional activities involved in leading any creative effort have an important, albeit often overlooked, implication. Those asked to lead creative efforts in firms are leading "organized chaos." And, leadership in chaotic settings is a particularly demanding, high-stress, high-risk form of leadership (DeChurch et al., 2011).

In fact, most creative efforts fail. And, even though firms need innovation, innovation based on creative work, failure can be costly. One implication of this observation is that leaders of creative efforts must be willing to tolerate risk and failure, often persisting despite initial failure. So why will leaders of creative efforts tolerate risk and failure? Again, we lack clear evidence in this regard. Nevertheless, the findings available to date suggest that three phenomena may underlie a leader's ability to tolerate risk and failure. First, they see, or forecast, a better future for the firm, their profession, and the world if things work out (O'Connor, 1998). Second, they are making an informed bet, or a set of bets, based on a portfolio of projects. Thus, while not every project will work out, some will. Third, they hope that they, their people, and the firm will learn, and will learn from failure, with respect to fundamentals bearing on the strategy and "business" of the firm. These observations are noteworthy because they suggest those leading the dynamic chaos that characterizes the leadership of creative efforts are ultimately pragmatists, albeit pragmatists who value learning and progressive product improvement (Mumford, 2002, 2006; Mumford & Van Doorn, 2001).

## 7.2 What Do They Need?

Our foregoing observations are noteworthy because they bring to fore a new question. What do those asked to lead creative efforts need to do their jobs? What knowledge, skills, and abilities are needed? Perhaps the most clear-cut conclusion to be drawn in this regard is that those asked to lead creative efforts cannot just be any manager the institution happens to select. Rather those asked to lead creative efforts need, they do not just need but also must have, substantial professional expertise (Barnowe, 1975). One cannot scan the professional environment and identify opportunities worth pursuing unless they have substantial expertise. One cannot intellectually stimulate followers unless they know why the project is professionally important. One cannot provide professionals with meaningful critical feedback unless they know the technology and/or profession. In this regard, however, it is not just "book learning" that provides the professional expertise needed by those asked to lead creative efforts. Rather, they need "hands on experience" and "bench skills" if they are to be able to plan project work and provide meaningful feedback (Mumford et al., 2001).

It is not just technical expertise those asked to lead creative efforts need, they also need expertise with respect to the firm and its areas of operation. Remember, leaders of creative efforts must "sell" the creative effort to the firm (Howell & Boies, 2004). And viable "sales" are based on an understanding of the firm and its business strategy. Moreover, leaders of creative efforts must help key support units not only to understand the implications of a potential new project, but also to deal with the implications of the creative work for *their* day-to-day operations. Thus, leaders of creative efforts need not only to understand firm strategy, they also need to know how the work gets done in the firm if they are to help others grapple with the practical implications of creative efforts. And, this kind of localized, firm specific, expertise takes time to acquire.

Although leaders' professional and firm expertise are critical for the success of creative projects, one must not lose sight of another capacity that is also critical. Leaders must give followers feedback on their work – compensatory feedback intended to improve the work. One implication of this observation is that leaders of creative efforts must think, and think deeply, about the work they are being presented with (Gibson & Mumford, 2013). Even more important, however, is that those who are asked to lead creative efforts must themselves be able to think creatively (Zaccaro et al., 2015). They must know how to define problems, gather information, combine approaches, and evaluate ideas. And, they must be able to identify critical causes, forecast likely outcomes, and analyze constraints (Mumford et al., 2017). These observations are noteworthy because they imply that leaders of creative efforts must themselves have substantial creative thinking skills to get the work done, sell the work to the firm, and engage followers in an intellectually stimulating task.

The leaders of creative efforts also need two other skills that are often easy to overlook. Creative work is done by people – people working in a social institution. Thus, those asked to lead creative efforts need social skills as well as technical skills (Chaney & Owens, 1964). These social skills, however, may be far more complex than we typically assume. Leaders must know how to establish and maintain a viable network of contacts within both the firm and the profession. They must be able to appraise and evaluate others with respect to their interests and concerns. In other words, they need some degree of emotional intelligence (Cherniss, 2001). Moreover, given the chaotic nature of creative efforts in firms, leaders will need both the capacity to reflect on themselves and the ability to reflect on others and their needs and concerns (Strange & Mumford, 2005).

Leaders' social and technical skills point to another key skill needed by those asked to lead creative efforts. Leaders of creative efforts must be good teachers and excellent communicators. Remember, leaders must develop followers professionally. They must lay out the implications of creative work for the more routine work being done in other units. Without teaching and communication skills, it is unlikely such efforts will be met with much success.

The importance of teaching skills, however, is noteworthy in another way. Creative work occurs in turbulent environments characterized by ongoing change – both technical change and change in firm practices (Hunter, Bedell, & Mumford, 2007). This point is noteworthy because it implies that the leaders of creative efforts must be actively engaged in ongoing professional development. Part of this professional development, of course, entails reflection, often self-reflection, on the work they and their people have done. Another part of this professional development, however, means staying up to date on the profession, its technologies, and its key issues. Thus, leaders of creative efforts will be actively engaged in the work and learning from the work. More centrally, and more critically, they will be actively engaged in their profession by seeking ongoing professional development.

## 7.3 Where Do They Come From?

We have already noted that leaders of creative efforts, at least effective leaders, must be experts in the field. They must be able to think creatively and in-depth about both their work and the firm. They must have substantial social skills – skills that include interactional skills, communication skills, and sales skills. They must be able to teach others and themselves. And, all of this must occur in a dynamic, chaotic environment where the leader seeks to synthesize, or integrate, the concerns of the profession, the firm, and their followers. These observations are noteworthy because they pose a question – a question of real importance to any firm seeking innovation, growth, and survival. Where do those people come from?

The long and short answer to this question is that we really do not know. A few qualitative studies indicate that extant leaders of creative efforts carefully attend to potential sources of leadership talent often relying on professional connections to identify these people (Gertner, 2012). There is also evidence which suggests that extant leaders pay special attention to monitoring the people they see as high potential future leaders (Zuckerman, 1979). Beyond these observations, however, we know very little.

Nonetheless, our foregoing observations suggest a number of actions that might be taken by firms to improve the cadre of people available to lead creative efforts. One clear-cut strategy is to systematically assess the personal qualities of relevant professionals (Arthur et al., 2003). What should be noted here, however, is that such assessments should not be based on the typical managerial assessment center. The leaders of creative efforts require a rather different skill profile – they must display creative thinking skills, planning skills, and constraint analysis skills, as well as sales skills, self-reflection skills, and the ability to intellectually stimulate others. Systematic assessments of these skills, especially systematic assessments of those skills coupled with developmental feedback, may prove of substantial value in developing creative leaders.

Developmental feedback derived from systematic assessment of the skills required for leading creative efforts has value for another technique that might prove useful. Knowing what a potential leader's strengths and weaknesses are provides a basis for identifying rotational assignments or developmental assignments (Campion, Cheraskin, & Stevens, 1994). For example, if an otherwise talented person has difficulty communicating ideas, they might be asked to brief relevant support units. Other rotational assignments, for example, a period providing training in support units, might prove valuable in helping high potential people develop requisite knowledge of the business as a whole.

Yet another way high-potential people might be developed is through formal training. Indeed, a case can be made that rotational assignments will prove most beneficial when training has been provided to people to ready them for such assignments. However, at least in one case, it has been found that well-developed, appropriately scaffolded training is beneficial in developing the kind of skills needed by those asked to lead creative efforts (Mumford et al., 2000).

Still another technique likely to prove of some value in developing a cadre of people capable of leading creative efforts may be found in organizational policies encouraging ongoing professional development. Firms that encourage publications, conference attendance, and membership in journal editorial boards are implementing policies likely to encourage the development and maintenance of the professional expertise needed to lead creative efforts. Such activities, however, serve not only to develop professional skills, they also serve to build the network of professional contacts that will be needed by those asked to lead creative efforts.

These observations are noteworthy because they suggest that a more systematic approach to the development of the potential for effective leadership of creative efforts is needed than one typically sees in most firms. And, one must remember that systematic leadership development programs are not inexpensive. Thus, firms may be willing to allow the development of leadership for creative efforts to amble along in an ad hoc fashion, hoping things will just somehow workout in the long run.

We would argue that this approach to developing those who will be asked to lead creative efforts is a tragic mistake. To survive, grow, and increase market share and profits, firms must innovate. While any given creative effort may, or may not, workout, ongoing learning with respect to firm fundamentals appears to increase the likelihood some creative efforts will succeed. And, given the impact of the success of creative efforts on firm success and survival, there seems to be ample reason for firms to invest in such systematic leader development efforts.

Indeed, such investments are likely to prove crucial because the available evidence indicates that effective leadership is perhaps the single most powerful force shaping the success of creative efforts in firms. And, over the years, as evident in this Element, we have developed a good understanding of exactly what is needed to lead creative efforts. Thus, the foundation exists that should allow firms to initiate such efforts with a real hope of success. We hope the present effort provides an impetus for future work along these lines.

# References

Acar, S., & Runco, M. A. (2012). Psychoticism and creativity: A meta-analytic review. *Psychology of Aesthetics, Creativity, and the Arts*, **6**, 341–350.

Allen, T. J., & Cohen, S. I. (1969). Information flow in research and development laboratories. *Administrative Science Quarterly*, **14**, 12–19.

Amabile, T. M. (1985). Motivation and creativity: Effects of motivational orientation on creative writers. *Journal of Personality and Social Psychology*, **48**, 393–399.

Amabile, T. M., Conti, R., Coon, H., Lazenby, J., & Herron, M. (1996). Assessing the work environment for creativity. *Academy of Management Journal*, **39**, 1154–1184.

Amabile, T., & Kramer, S. (2011a). *The progress principle: Using small wins to ignite joy, engagement, and creativity at work*. Boston, MA: Harvard Business Review Press.

Amabile, T. M., & Kramer, S. J. (2011b). Meeting the challenges of a person-centric work psychology. *Industrial and Organizational Psychology*, **4**, 116–121.

Amabile, T. M., Schatzel, E. A., Moneta, G. B., & Kramer, S. J. (2004). Leader behavior and the work environment for creativity: Perceived leader support. *The Leadership Quarterly*, **15**, 5–32.

Anacona, D. G., & Caldwell, D. F. (1992). Bridging the boundary: External activity and performance in organizational teams. *Administrative Science Quarterly*, **37**, 634–665.

Anacona, D. G., & Caldwell, D. F. (1998). Rethinking team composition from the outside in. In D. H. Gruenfeld (Ed.), *Research on managing groups and teams, Vol. 1: Composition* (pp. 21–37). Greenwhich, CT: Elsevier.

Andersen, H., Barker, P., & Chen, X. (2006). *The cognitive structure of scientific revolutions*. New York, NY: Cambridge University Press.

Arthur Jr., W., Day, E. A., McNelly, T. L., & Edens, P. S. (2003). A meta-analysis of the criterion-related validity of assessment center dimensions. *Personnel Psychology*, **56**, 125–153.

Atwater, L., & Carmeli, A. (2009). Leader–member exchange, feelings of energy, and involvement in creative work. *The Leadership Quarterly*, **20**, 264–275.

Baer, M., Leenders, R. A. J., Oldham, G. R., & Vadera, A. K. (2010). Win or lose the battle for creativity: The power and perils of intergroup competition. *Academy of Management Journal*, **53**, 827–845.

Baker, D. D., & Ganster, D. C. (1985). Leader communication style: A test of average versus vertical dyad linkage models. *Group & Organization Studies*, **10**, **242–259**.

Barbuto Jr, J. E., & Wheeler, D. W. (2006). Scale development and construct clarification of servant leadership. *Group & Organization Management*, **31**, **300–326**.

Barnowe, J. T. (1975). Leadership and performance outcomes in research organizations: The supervisor of scientists as a source of assistance. *Organizational Behavior & Human Performance*, **14**, **264–280**.

Bass, B. M. (1997). Does the transactional-transformational leadership paradigm transcend organizational and national boundaries? *American Psychologist*, **52**, **130–139**.

Bass, B. M., & Avolio, B. J. (1990). The implications of transactional and transformational leadership for individual, team, and organizational development. In W. Pasmore & R. W. Woodman (Eds.), *Research in organizational change and development* (pp. **231–272**). Greenwich, CT: JAI Press.

Bass, B. M., & Bass, R. (2008). *The bass handbook of leadership: Theory, research, and managerial applications*. New York: The Free Press.

Baughman, W. A., & Mumford, M. D. (1995). Process-analytic models of creative capacities: Operations involved in the combination and reorganization process. *Creativity Research Journal*, **9**, **63–76**.

Beghetto, R. A., & Karwowski, M. (2017). Toward untangling creative-self beliefs. In M. Karwowski & J. C. Kaufman (Eds.), *The creative self: Effect of beliefs, self-efficacy, mindset, and identity* (pp. **3–22**). New York: Elsevier.

Bennich-Björkman, L. (2017). Academic leadership: Embracing uncertainty and diversity by building communication and trust. In M. D. Mumford & S. Hemlin (Eds.), *Handbook of research on leadership and creativity* (pp. **419–434**). Northhampton, MA: Edward Elgar.

Bergek, A., Jacobsson, S., & Sandén, B. A. (2008). "Legitimation" and "development of positive externalities": Two key processes in the formation phase of technological innovation systems. *Technology Analysis & Strategic Management*, **20**, **575–592**.

Berger, R., Dutta, S., Raffel, T., & Samuels, G. (2009). *Innovating at the top: How global CEOs drive innovation for growth and profit*. London, UK: Palgrave Macmillan.

Besemer, S. P., & O'Quin, K. (1998). Creative product analysis matrix: Testing the model structure and a comparison among products – three novel chairs. *Creativity Research Journal*, **11**, **333–346**.

Bessen, J., & Maskin, E. (2009). Sequential innovation, patents, and imitation. *The RAND Journal of Economics*, **40**, 611–635.

Bird, K., & Sherwin, M. J. (2005). *American prometheus: The triumph and tragedy of J. Robert Oppenheimer.* New York: Knopf.

Blair, C. S., & Mumford, M. D. (2007). Errors in idea evaluation: Preference for the unoriginal? *The Journal of Creative Behavior*, **41**, 197–222.

Boer, H., & During, W. E. (2001). Innovation, what innovation? A comparison between product, process and organisational innovation. *International Journal of Technology Management*, **22**, 83–107.

Boies, K., Fiset, J., & Gill, H. (2015). Communication and trust are key: Unlocking the relationship between leadership and team performance and creativity. *The Leadership Quarterly*, **26**, 1080–1094.

Bonet, D. (2001). *The business of listening: A practical guide to effective listening.* Crisp Learning.

Braun, S., Peus, C., Weisweiler, S., & Frey, D. (2013). Transformational leadership, job satisfaction, and team performance: A multilevel mediation model of trust. *The Leadership Quarterly*, **24**, 270–283.

Bronzini, R., & Piselli, P. (2016). The impact of R&D subsidies on firm innovation. *Research Policy*, **45**, 442–457.

Byrne, C. L., Shipman, A. S., & Mumford, M. D. (2010). The effects of forecasting on creative problem-solving: An experimental study. *Creativity Research Journal*, **22**, 119–138.

Cacioppo, J. T., Petty, R. E., & Kao, C. F. (1984). The efficient assessment of need for cognition. *Journal of Personality Assessment*, **48**, 306–307.

Cai, W., Lysova, E. I., Bossink, B. A. G., Khapova, S. N., & Wang, W. (2019). Psychological capital and self-reported employee creativity: The moderating role of supervisor support and job characteristics. *Creativity and Innovation Management*, **28**, 30–41.

Calantone, R. J., Cavusgil, S. T., & Zhao, Y. (2002). Learning orientation, firm innovation capability, and firm performance. *Industrial Marketing Management*, **31**, 515–524.

Caldwell, D. F., & O'Reilly III, C. A. (2003). The determinants of team-based innovation in organizations: The role of social influence. *Small Group Research*, **34**, 497–517.

Campion, M. A., Cheraskin, L., & Stevens, M. J. (1994). Career-related antecedents and outcomes of job rotation. *Academy of Management Journal*, **37**, 1518–1542.

Cao, Q., Simsek, Z., & Zhang, H. (2010). Modelling the joint impact of the CEO and the TMT on organizational ambidexterity. *Journal of Management Studies*, **47**, 1272–1296.

Carmeli, A., Gelbard, R., & Reiter-Palmon, R. (2013). Leadership, creative problem-solving capacity, and creative performance: The importance of knowledge sharing. *Human Resource Management*, **52**, **95–121**.

Carmeli, A., Reiter-Palmon, R., & Ziv, E. (2010). Inclusive leadership and employee involvement in creative tasks in the workplace: The mediating role of psychological safety. *Creativity Research Journal*, **22**, **250–260**.

Carter, S. M., & West, M. A. (1998). Reflexivity, effectiveness, and mental health in BBC-TV production teams. *Small Group Research*, **29**, **583–601**.

Caughron, J. J., & Mumford, M. D. (2008). Project planning: The effects of using formal planning techniques on creative problem-solving. *Creativity and Innovation Management*, **17**, **204–215**.

Cefis, E., & Marsili, O. (2005). A matter of life and death: Innovation and firm survival. *Industrial and Corporate Change*, **14**, **1167–1192**.

Černe, M., Jaklič, M., & Škerlavaj, M. (2013). Authentic leadership, creativity, and innovation: A multilevel perspective. *Leadership*, **9**, **63–85**.

Chandy, R. K., & Tellis, G. J. (1998). Organizing for radical product innovation: The overlooked role of willingness to cannibalize. *Journal of Marketing Research*, **35**, **474–487**.

Chandy, R. K., & Tellis, G. J. (2000). The incumbent's curse? Incumbency, size and radical innovation. *Journal of Marketing*, **64**, **1–17**.

Chaney, F. B., & Owens, W. A. (1964). Life history antecedents of sales, research, and general engineering interest. *Journal of Applied Psychology*, **48**, **101–105**.

Chang, S. C., & Lee, M. S. (2007). A study on relationship among leadership, organizational culture, the operation of learning organization and employees' job satisfaction. *The Learning Organization*, **14**, **155–185**.

Chen, L., Zheng, W., Yang, B., & Bai, S. (2016). Transformational leadership, social capital and organizational innovation. *Leadership & Organization Development Journal*, **37(7)**, **843–859**.

Chen, M. H. (2006). Understanding the benefits and detriments of conflict on team creativity process. *Creativity and Innovation Management*, **15**, **105–116**.

Cherniss, C. (2001). Emotional intelligence and organizational effectiveness. In C. Cherniss & D. Goleman (Eds.), *The emotionally intelligent workplace* (pp. **3–12**). San Francisco, CA: Jossey-Bass.

Cheung, M. F., & Wong, C. S. (2011). Transformational leadership, leader support, and employee creativity. *Leadership & Organization Development Journal*, **32(7)**, **656–672**.

Christiaans, H. H. (2002). Creativity as a design criterion. *Communication Research Journal*, **14**, **41–54**.

Clydesdale, G. (2006). Creativity and competition: The beatles. *Creativity Research Journal*, **18**, **129–139**.

Cohen-Charash, Y., & Spector, P. E. (2001). The role of justice in organizations: A meta-analysis: Erratum. *Organizational Behavior and Human Decision Processes*, **86(2), 278–321**.

Connelly, M. S., Gilbert, J. A., Zaccaro, S. J. et al. (2000). Exploring the relationship of leadership skills and knowledge to leader performance. *The Leadership Quarterly*, **11, 65–86**.

Cooper, R. G., & Kleinschmidt, E. J. (1995). Benchmarking the firm's critical success factors in new product development. *Journal of Product Innovation Management: An International Publication of the Product Development & Management Association*, **12, 374–391**.

Daellenbach, U. S., McCarthy, A. M., & Schoenecker, T. S. (1999). Commitment to innovation: The impact of top management team characteristics. *R&D Management*, **29, 199–208**.

Damanpour, F. (1991). Organizational innovation: A meta-analysis of effects of determinants and moderators. *Academy of Management Journal*, **34, 555–590**.

Damanpour, F., & Aravind, D. (2012). Managerial innovation: Conceptions, processes, and antecedents. *Management and Organization Review*, **8, 423–454**.

Davison, G., & Blackman, B. (2005). The role of mental models in innovative teams. *European Journal of Innovation Management*, **8, 409–423**.

Day, D. V., Riggio, R. E., & Mulligan, R. Y. (2020). Leadership and monitoring skills. In M. D. Mumford & C. A. Higgs (Eds.), *Leader thinking skills: Capacities for contemporary leadership* (pp. **340–361**). New York, NY: Taylor and Francis.

De Dreu, C. K. (2002). Team innovation and team effectiveness: The importance of minority dissent and reflexivity. *European Journal of Work and Organizational Psychology*, **11, 285–298**.

De Dreu, C. K. (2006). When too little or too much hurts: Evidence for a curvilinear relationship between task conflict and innovation in teams. *Journal of Management*, **32, 83–107**.

DeChurch, L. A., Burke, C. S., Shuffler, M. L. et al. (2011). A historiometric analysis of leadership in mission critical multiteam environments. *The Leadership Quarterly*, **22, 152–169**.

DeRosa, D. M., Smith, C. L., & Hantula, D. A. (2007). The medium matters: Mining the long-promised merit of group interaction in creative idea generation tasks in a meta-analysis of the electronic group brainstorming literature. *Computers and Human Behavior*, **23, 1549–1581**.

Dewey, J. (1910). *How we think*. Lexington, MA: D. C. Heath.

Diehl, M., & Stroebe, W. (1987). Productivity loss in brainstorming groups: Toward the solution of a riddle. *Journal of Personality and Social Psychology*, **53**, 497–509.

Dong, Y., Bartol, K. M., Zhang, Z. X., & Li, C. (2017). Enhancing employee creativity via individual skill development and team knowledge sharing: Influences of dual-focused transformational leadership. *Journal of Organizational Behavior*, **38**, 439–458.

Dougherty, D., Borrelli, L., Munir, K., & O'Sullivan, A. (2000). Systems of organizational sensemaking for sustained product innovation. *Journal of Engineering and Technology Management*, **17**, 321–355.

Dougherty, D., & Hardy, B. F. (1996a). Sustained innovation production in large mature organizations: Overcoming organization problems. *Academy of Management Journal*, **39**, 826–851.

Dougherty, D., & Hardy, C. (1996b). Sustained product innovation in large, mature organizations: Overcoming innovation-to-organization problems. *Academy of Management Journal*, **39**, 1120–1152.

Drazin, R., Glynn, M. A., & Kazanjian, R. K. (1999). Multilevel theorizing about creativity in organizations: A sensemaking perspective. *Academy of Management Review*, **24**, 286–307.

Eisenbeiss, S. A., & Boerner, S. (2013). A double-edged sword: Transformational leadership and individual creativity. *British Journal of Management*, **24**, 54–68.

Eisenbeiss, S. A., Van Knippenberg, D., & Boerner, S. (2008). Transformational leadership and team innovation: Integrating team climate principles. *Journal of Applied Psychology*, **93**, 1438–1446.

Eisenberger, R., & Shanock, L. (2003). Rewards, intrinsic motivation, and creativity: A case study of conceptual and methodological isolation. *Creativity Research Journal*, **15**, 121–130.

Ekvall, G., & Ryhammar, L. (1999). The creative climate: Its determinants and effects at a Swedish University. *Creativity Research Journal*, **12**, 303–310.

Ericsson, K. A., & Charness, N. (1994). Expert performance: Its structure and acquisition. *American Psychologist*, **49**, 725–747.

Ericsson, K. A., & Charness, N. (1999). Becoming an expert: Training or talent? In S. J. Ceci & W. M. Williams (Eds.), *The nature–nurture debate: The essential readings* (pp. **200**–**255**). Malden, MA: Blackwell.

Farris, G. F. (1972). The effect of individual role on performance in innovative groups. *R & D Management*, **3**, 23–28.

Feist, G. J. (1998). A meta-analysis of personality in scientific and artistic creativity. *Personality and Social Psychological Review*, **2**, 290–309.

Feist, G. J., & Gorman, M. E. (1998). The psychology of science: Review and integration of a nascent discipline. *Review of General Psychology*, **2**, 3–47.

Fleishman, E. A., Mumford, M. D., Zaccaro, S. J. et al. (1991). Taxonomic efforts in the description of leader behavior: A synthesis and functional interpretation. *The Leadership Quarterly*, **2**, **245–287**.

Ford, C. M. (1996). A theory of individual creative action in multiple social domains. *Academy of Management Review*, **21**, **1112–1142**.

Ford, C. M., Sharfman, M. P., & Dean, J. W. (2008). Factors associated with creative strategic decisions. *Creativity and Innovation Management*, **17**, **171–185**.

Friedrich, T. L., & Mumford, M. D. (2009). The effects of conflicting information on creative thought: A source of performance improvements or decrements? *Creativity Research Journal*, **21**, **265–281**.

Furnham, A. (2020). Personality and creativity at work. In M. D. Mumford & E. M. Todd (Eds.), *Creativity and innovation in organizations* (pp. **89–104**). New York: Taylor & Francis.

Gabler, N. (2007). *Walt Disney: The biography*. London, UK: White Lion.

Gertner, J. (2012). *The idea factory: Bell Labs and the great age of American innovation*. London, UK: Penguin.

Gibson, C., & Mumford, M. D. (2013). Evaluation, criticism, and creativity: Criticism content and effects on creative problem solving. *Psychology of Aesthetics, Creativity, and the Arts*, **7**, **314–331**.

Gilson, L. L., & Shalley, C. E. (2004). A little creativity goes a long way: An examination of teams' engagement in creative processes. *Journal of Management*, **30**, **453–470**.

Giorgini, V., & Mumford, M. D. (2013). Backup plans and creative problem-solving: Effects of causal, error, and resource processing. *The International Journal of Creativity and Problem Solving*, **23**, **121–146**.

Goh, S., & Richards, G. (1997). Benchmarking the learning capability of organizations. *European Management Journal*, **15**, **575–583**.

Guilford, J. P. (1950). Creativity. *American Psychologist*, **5**, **444–454**.

Gumusluoglu, L., & Ilsev, A. (2009). Transformational leadership, creativity, and organizational innovation. *Journal of Business Research*, **62**, **461–473**.

Hadjikosta, K., & Friedrich, T. (2020). Creativity and innovation in the context of firms. In M. D. Mumford & E. M. Todd (Eds.), *Creativity and innovation in organizations* (pp. **271–314**). New York: Taylor & Francis.

Hambrick, D. C. (2015). Top management teams. *Wiley Encyclopedia of Management*, *11*, **1–2**.

Hardy III, J. H., Ness, A. M., & Mecca, J. (2017). Outside the box: Epistemic curiosity as a predictor of creative problem-solving and creative performance. *Personality and Individual Differences*, **104**, 230–237.

Hegarty, W. H., & Hoffman, R. C. (1990). Product/market innovations: A study of top management involvement among four cultures. *Journal of Product Innovation Management: An International Publication of the Product Development & Management Association*, **7**, 186–199.

Hemlin, S. (2009). Creative knowledge environments: An interview study with group members and group leaders of university and industry R&D groups in biotechnology. *Creativity and Innovation Management*, **18**, 278–285.

Hemlin, S., & Olsson, L. (2011). Creativity-stimulating leadership: A critical incident study of leaders' influence on creativity in research groups. *Creativity and Innovation Management*, **20**, 49–58.

Hennessey, B. A., & Amabile, T. M. (1998). Reality, intrinsic motivation, and creativity. *American Psychologist*, **53(6), 674–675**.

Hill, R. C., & Levenhagen, M. (1995). Metaphors and mental models: Sensemaking and sensegiving in innovative and entrepreneurial activities. *Journal of Management*, **21, 1057–1074**.

Hirst, G., Van Knippenberg, D., Zhou, J., Quintane, E., & Zhu, C. (2015). Heard it through the grapevine: Indirect networks and employee creativity. *Journal of Applied Psychology*, **100(2), 567–574**.

Hounshell, D. (1992). Du Pont and the management of large-scale research and development. In P. Gallison & B. Hevly (Eds.), *Big science: The growth of large-scale research* (pp. **236–264**). Redwood City, CA: Stanford University Press.

Howell, J. M., & Boies, K. (2004). Champions of technological innovation: The influences of contextual knowledge, role orientation, idea generation, and idea promotion on champion emergence. *The Leadership Quarterly*, **15, 130–149**.

Howell, J. M., & Higgins, C. A. (1990). Leadership behaviors, influence tactics, and career experiences of champions of technological innovation. *The Leadership Quarterly*, **1, 249–264**.

Howell, J. M., & Shea, C. M. (2006). Effects of champion behavior, team potency, and external communication activities on predicting team performance. *Group & Organization Management*, **31, 180–211**.

Howitt, P., & Aghion, P. (1998). Capital accumulation and innovation as complementary factors in long-run growth. *Journal of Economic Growth*, **3, 111–130**.

Huber, G. (1998). Synergies between organizational learning and creativity & innovation. *Creativity and Innovation Management*, **7, 3–8**.

Hughes, D. J., Lee, A., Tian, A. W., Newman, A., & Legood, A. (2018). Leadership, creativity, and innovation: A critical review and practical recommendations. *The Leadership Quarterly*, **29**, **549–569**.

Hughes, T. P. (1989). *American genesis: A history of the American genius for invention*. New York: Penguin.

Hülsheger, U. R., Anderson, N., & Salgado, J. F. (2009). Team-level predictors of innovation at work: A comprehensive meta-analysis spanning three decades of research. *Journal of Applied Psychology*, **94(5)**, **1128**.

Hunter, S. T., Bedell, K. E., & Mumford, M. D. (2005). Dimensions of creative climate: A general taxonomy. *Korean Journal of Thinking & Problem Solving*, **15(2)**, **97–116**.

Hunter, S. T., Bedell, K. E., & Mumford, M. D. (2007). Climate for creativity: A quantitative review. *Creativity Research Journal*, **19**, **69–90**.

Hunter, S. T., Bedell-Avers, K. E., Hunsicker, C. M., Mumford, M. D., & Ligon, G. S. (2008). Applying multiple knowledge structures in creative thought: Effects on idea generation and problem-solving. *Creativity Research Journal*, **20**, **137–154**.

Hunter, S. T., Farr, J. L., Heinen, R. L., & Allen, J. B. (2019). Integrating creative climate and creative problem-solving. In M. D. Mumford & E. M. Todd (Eds.), *Creativity and innovation in organizations* (pp. **143–166**). London: Routledge.

Hunter, S. T., Neely Jr, B. H., & Gutworth, M. B. (2018). Selection and team creativity: Meeting unique challenges through diversity and flexibility. In R. Reiter-Palmon (Ed.), *Team creativity and innovation* (pp. **259–281**). Oxford, UK: Oxford University Press.

Isaacson, W. (2011). *Steve Jobs*. New York: Simon & Schuster.

Jacobs, T. O., & Jaques, E. (1991). Executive leadership. In R. Gal & A. D. Mangelsdorf (Eds.), *Handbook of military psychology* (pp. **431–447**). Chichester: Wiley.

Jaiswal, N. K., & Dhar, R. L. (2017). The influence of servant leadership, trust in leader and thriving on employee creativity. *Leadership & Organization Development Journal*, **38**, **2–21**.

James, L. R., James, L. A., & Ashe, D. K. (1990). The meaning of organizations: The role of cognition and values. In B. Schneider (Ed.), *Organizational climate and culture* (pp. **40–84**). San Francisco, CA: Jossey-Bass.

Jassawalla, A. R., & Sashittal, H. C. (1999). Building collaborative cross-functional new product teams. *Academy of Management Perspectives*, **13**, **50–63**.

Jaussi, K. S., & Dionne, S. D. (2003). Leading for creativity: The role of unconventional behavior. *The Leadership Quarterly*, **14**, **351–368**.

Jelinek, M., & Schoonhoven, C. B. (1990). *The innovation marathon: Lessons from high technology firms*. San Francisco, CA: Jossey-Bass.

Karwowski, M. (2011). It doesn't hurt to ask … But sometimes it hurts to believe: Polish students' creative self-efficacy and its predictors. *Psychology of Aesthetics, Creativity, and the Arts*, **5**, **154–164**.

Katz, D., & Kahn, R. L. (1978). *The social psychology of organizations*. New York: Wiley.

Keller, R. T. (2001). Cross-functional project groups in research and new product development: Diversity, communications, job stress, and outcomes. *Academy of Management Journal*, **44**, **547–553**.

Keller, R. T. (2006). Transformational leadership, initiating structure, and substitutes for leadership: A longitudinal study of research and development project team performance. *Journal of Applied Psychology*, **91(1)**, **202–210**.

Khalili, A. (2016). Linking transformational leadership, creativity, innovation, and innovation-supportive climate. *Management Decision*, **10**, **111–125**.

Kickul, J., & Gundry, L. K. (2001). Breaking through boundaries for organizational innovation: New managerial roles and practices in e-commerce firms. *Journal of Management*, **27**, **347–361**.

Kidder, T. (1981). *The soul of a new machine*. New York: Avon.

Kogut, B., & Zander, U. (1996). What firms do? Coordination, identity, and learning. *Organization Science*, **7**, **502–518**.

Kolodner, J. L. (1997). Educational implications of analogy: A view from case-based reasoning. *American Psychologist*, **52(1)**, **57–66**.

Kozbelt, A. (2007). A quantitative analysis of Beethoven as self-critic: Implications for psychological theories of musical creativity. *Psychology of Music*, **35**, **144–168**.

Kratzer, J., Leenders, O. T. A., & Van Engelen, J. M. (2004). Stimulating the potential: Creative performance and communication in innovation teams. *Creativity and Innovation Management*, **13**, **63–71**.

Kratzer, J., Leenders, R. T. A., & Van Engelen, J. M. (2006). Team polarity and creative performance in innovation teams. *Creativity and Innovation Management*, **15**, **96–104**.

LaPierre, J., & Giroux, V. (2003). Creativity and work environment in a high-tech context. *Creativity and Work Environment*, **12**, **11–23**.

Lee, J. (2008). Effects of leadership and leader-member exchange on innovativeness. *Journal of Managerial Psychology*, **23**, **670–687**.

Lee, J. H. (**2015**). The effects of authentic leadership on organizational commitment, task performance and creative behavior. Unpublished doctoral dissertation. *Sungkyunkwan University*.

Lee-Kelley, L., & Blackman, D. (2005). In addition to shared goals: The impact of mental models on team innovation and learning. *International Journal of Innovation and Learning*, **2(1), 11–25**.

Licuanan, B. F., Dailey, L. R., & Mumford, M. D. (2007). Idea evaluation: Error in evaluating highly original ideas. *The Journal of Creative Behavior*, **41**, 1–27.

Liu, D., Chen, X. P., & Yao, X. (2011). From autonomy to creativity: A multilevel investigation of the mediating role of harmonious passion. *Journal of Applied Psychology*, **96(2), 294–309**.

Lonergan, D. C., Scott, G. M., & Mumford, M. D. (2004). Evaluative aspects of creative thought: Effects of idea appraisal and revision standards. *Creativity Research Journal*, **16, 231–246**.

Lu, S., Bartol, K. M., Venkataramani, V., Zheng, X., & Liu, X. (2019). Pitching novel ideas to the boss: The interactive effects of employees' idea enactment and influence tactics on creativity assessment and implementation. *Academy of Management Journal*, **62, 579–606**.

Maccurtain, S., Flood, P. C., Ramamoorty, N., West, M., & Dawson, J. (2009, August). The top team, trust, reflexivity, knowledge sharing and innovation. In *Academy of Management Proceedings* (Vol. 2009, No. 1, pp. **1–6**). Briarcliff Manor, NY 10510: Academy of Management.

Maier, N. R., & Solem, A. R. (1970). Improving solutions by turning choice situations into problems. In N. R. Maier (Ed.), *Problem solving and creativity: In groups and individuals* (pp. **390–395**). Belmont, CA: Books/Cole.

Majchrzak, A., More, P. H., & Faraj, S. (2012). Transcending knowledge differences in cross-functional teams. *Organization Science*, **23, 951–970**.

Mannix, E., & Neale, M. A. (2005). What differences make a difference? The promise and reality of diverse teams in organizations. *Psychological Science in the Public Interest*, **6, 31–55**.

March, J. G. (1991). Exploration and exploitation in organizational learning. *Organization Science*, **2, 71–87**.

Marcy, R. T., & Mumford, M. D. (2007). Social innovation: Enhancing creative performance through causal analysis. *Creativity Research Journal*, **19, 123–140**.

Marcy, R. T., & Mumford, M. D. (2010). Leader cognition: Improving leader performance through causal analysis. *The Leadership Quarterly*, **21, 1–19**.

Markham, S. E., & Smith, J. W. (2017). How can we advise Achilles? A rehabilitation of the concept of the champion for leadership. In M. D. Mumford & S. Hemlin (Eds.), *Handbook of research on leadership and creativity* (pp. **54–81**). London: Edward Elgar.

Markham, S. K. (2000). Corporate championing and antagonism as forms of political behavior: An R&D perspective. *Organization Science*, **11**, 429–447.

Markham, S. K., & Aiman-Smith, L. (2001). Product champions: Truths, myths and management. *Research-Technology Management*, **44**, 44–50.

Marta, S., Leritz, L. E., & Mumford, M. D. (2005). Leadership skills and group performance: Situational demands, behavioral requirements, and planning. *The Leadership Quarterly*, **16**, 97–120.

McClelland, D. C. (1961). *The achieving society*. New York: MacMillan.

McCrae, R. (1987). Creativity, divergent thinking, and openness to experience. *Journal of Personality and Social Psychology*, **52(6)**, **1258–1265**.

McDonough III, E. F. (2000). Investigation of factors contributing to the success of cross-functional teams. *Journal of Product Innovation Management: An International Publication of the Product Development & Management Association*, **17**, **221–235**.

McGill, M. E., Slocum Jr, J. W., & Lei, D. (1992). Management practices in learning organizations. *Organizational Dynamics*, **21**, 5–17.

McGonagle, J. J., & Vella, C. M. (2012). *Proactive intelligence: The successful executive's guide to intelligence*. London: Springer.

McIntosh, T., Mulhearn, T. J., & Mumford, M. D. (2021). Taking the good with the bad: The impact of forecasting timing and valence on idea evaluation and creativity. *Psychology of Aesthetics, Creativity, and the Arts*, **15**, **111–124**.

McKay, A. S., & Kaufman, J. C. (2020). The assessment of creative and innovative performance. In M. D. Mumford & E. M. Todd (Eds.), *Creativity and innovation in organizations* (pp. **17–40**). New York: Taylor and Francis.

Medeiros, K. E., Partlow, P. J., & Mumford, M. D. (2014). Not too much, not too little: The influence of constraints on creative problem-solving. *Psychology of Aesthetics, Creativity, and the Arts*, **8**, **198–210**.

Medeiros, K. E., Steele, L. M., Watts, L. L., & Mumford, M. D. (2018). Timing is everything: Examining the role of constraints throughout the creative process. *Psychology of Aesthetics, Creativity, and the Arts*, **12**, **471–488**.

Meindl, J. R. (1995). The romance of leadership as a follower-centric theory: A social constructionist approach. *The Leadership Quarterly*, **6**, **329–341**.

Miles, R. E., & Snow, C. C. (1978). *Organizational strategy, structure and process*. New York: McGraw-Hill.

Miron-Spektor, E., Erez, M., & Naveh, E. (2011). The effect of conformist and attentive-to-detail members on team innovation: Reconciling the innovation paradox. *Academy of Management Journal*, **54**, 740–760.

Mullen, B., Johnson, C., & Salas, E. (1991). Productivity loss in brainstorming groups: A meta-analytic integration. *Basic and Applied Social Psychology*, **12**, **3–23**.

Mumford, M. D. (2000). Managing creative people: Strategies and tactics for innovation. *Human Resource Management Review*, **10**, **1–29**.

Mumford, M. D. (2002). Social innovation: Ten cases from Benjamin Franklin. *Creativity Research Journal*, **14**, **253–266**.

Mumford, M. D. (2006). *Pathways to outstanding leadership: A comparative analysis of charismatic, ideological and pragmatic leaders*. Mahwah, NJ: Erlbaum.

Mumford, M. D., Baughman, W. A., Threlfall, K. V., Supinski, E. P., & Costanza, D. P. (1996). Process-based measures of creative problem-solving skills: I. Problem construction. *Creativity Research Journal*, **9**, **63–76**.

Mumford, M. D., Bedell-Avers, K. E., & Hunter, S. T. (2008). Planning for innovation: A multi-level perspective. In M. D. Mumford, S. T. Hunter, & K. E. Bedell-Avers (Eds.), *Research in multi-level issues, Vol. 7: Multi-level issues in creativity and innovation* (pp. **107–154**). Oxford: Elsevier.

Mumford, M. D., Connelly, M. S., Scott, G. M. et al. (2005). Career experiences and scientific performance: A study of social, physical, life, and health sciences. *Creativity Research Journal*, **17**, **105–129**.

Mumford, M. D., Durban, C., Gujar, Y., Buck, J., & Todd, E. M. (2018). Leading creative efforts: Common functions and common skills. In C. Mainemelis, O. Epitropaki, & R. Kark (Eds.), *Creative leadership* (pp. **59–78**). London, UK: Routledge.

Mumford, M. D., Feldman, J. M., Hein, M. B., & Nago, D. J. (2001). Tradeoffs between ideas and structure: Individual versus group performance in creative problem-solving. *Journal of Creative Behavior*, **35**, **1–23**.

Mumford, M. D., & Fichtel, M. W. (2021). Local safety versus global risk: Models of creative work environments. In R. Reiter-Palmon (Ed.), *Creativity at work* (pp. **99–107**). London, UK: Palgrave Macmillan.

Mumford, M. D., Friedrich, T. L., Caughron, J. J., & Antes, A. L. (2009). Leadership research: Traditions, developments, and current directions. In D. A. Buchanan & A. Bryman (Eds.), *The Sage handbook of organizational research methods* (pp. **111–127**). Thousand Oaks, CA: Sage.

Mumford, M. D., Friedrich, T. L., Caughron, J. J., & Byrne, C. L. (2007). Leader cognition in real-world settings: How do leaders think about crises? *The Leadership Quarterly*, **18**, **515–543**.

Mumford, M. D., & Gustafson, S. B. (2007). Creative thought: Cognition and problem-solving in a dynamic system. In M. A. Runco (Ed.), *Creativity research handbook, Vol. 11* (pp. **33–77**). Creskill, NJ: Hampton.

Mumford, M. D., Hester, K. S., Robledo, I. C. et al. (2012). Mental models and creative problem-solving: The relationship of objective and subjective model attributes. *Creativity Research Journal*, **24**, **311–330**.

Mumford, M. D., & Hunter, S. T. (2005). Innovation in organizations: A multi-level perspective on creativity. In F. J. Yammarino & F. Dansereau (Eds.), *Research in multi-level issues, Vol. 4* (pp. **11–74**). Oxford: Elsevier.

Mumford, M. D., & Licuanan, B. (2004). Leading for innovation: Conclusions, issues, and directions. *The Leadership Quarterly*, **15**, **163–171**.

Mumford, M. D., Marks, M. A., Connelly, M. S., Zaccaro, S. J., & Reiter-Palmon, R. (2000). Development of leadership skills: Experience and timing. *The Leadership Quarterly*, **11**, **87–114**.

Mumford, M. D., Martin, R., Elliott, S., & McIntosh, T. (2019). Leading for creativity: A tripartite model. In R. J. Sternberg & J. Kaufman (Eds.), *The Cambridge handbook of creativity* (pp. **546–566**). Cambridge: Cambridge University Press.

Mumford, M. D., Martin, R., Elliott, S., & McIntosh, T. (2020). Creative failure: Why can't people solve creative problems. *The Journal of Creative Behavior*, **54**, **378–394**.

Mumford, M. D., Mecca, J. T., & Watts, L. L. (2015). Planning processes: Relevant cognitive operations. In M. D. Mumford & M. Frese (Eds.), *The psychology of planning in organizations: Research and applications* (pp. **9–30**). Milton Park, UK: Taylor & Francis.

Mumford, M. D., Mobley, M. I., Uhlman, C. E., Reiter-Palmon, R., & Doares, L. (1991). Process analytic models of creative capacities. *Creativity Research Journal*, **4**, **91–122**.

Mumford, M. D., & Mulhearn, T. J. (2019). Leading creative research and development efforts: A literature review and proposed framework for the engineering domain. *Proceedings of the Institution of Mechanical Engineers, Part C: Journal of Mechanical Engineering Science*, **233**, **403–414**.

Mumford, M. D., Mulhearn, T. J., Watts, L. L., Steele, L., & McIntosh, T. J. (2018). Leader impacts on creative teams: Direction, engagement, and sales. In R. Reiter-Palmon (Ed.), *Team creativity and innovation* (pp. **131–166**). New York: Oxford University Press.

Mumford, M. D., Schultz, R. A., & Van Doorn, J. R. (2001). Performance in planning: Processes, requirements, and errors. *Review of General Psychology*, **5**, **213–240**.

Mumford, M. D., Scott, G. M., Gaddis, B., & Strange, J. M. (2002). Leading creative people: Orchestrating expertise and relationships. *The Leadership Quarterly*, **13**, **705–750**.

Mumford, M. D., Supinski, E. P., Baughman, W. A., Costanza, D. P., & Threlfall, K. V. (1997). Process-based measures of creative problem-solving skills: I. Overall prediction. *Creativity Research Journal*, **10**, 77–85.

Mumford, M. D., Todd, E. M., Higgs, C., & McIntosh, T. (2017). Cognitive skills and leadership performance: The nine critical skills. *The Leadership Quarterly*, **28**, 24–39.

Mumford, M. D., & Van Doorn, J. R. (2001). The leadership of pragmatism: Reconsidering Franklin in the age of charisma. *The Leadership Quarterly*, **12**, 274–309.

Mumford, M. D., Zaccaro, S. J., Harding, F. D., Jacobs, T. O., & Fleishman, E. A. (2000). Leadership skills for a changing world: Solving complex social problems. *The Leadership Quarterly*, **11**, 11–35.

Naidoo, V. (2010). Firm survival through a crisis: The influence of market orientation, marketing innovation and business strategy. *Industrial Marketing Management*, **39**, 1311-1320.

Nijstad, B. A., Berger-Selman, F., & De Dreu, C. K. (2014). Innovation in top management teams: Minority dissent, transformational leadership, and radical innovations. *European Journal of Work and Organizational Psychology*, **23**, 310–322.

Nohria, N., & Gulati, R. (1996). Is slack good or bad for innovation? *Academy of Management Journal*, **39**, 1245–1264.

Norrgren, F., & Schaller, J. (1999). Leadership style: Its impact on cross-functional product development. *Journal of Product Innovation Management: An International Publication of the Product Development & Management Association*, **16**, 377–384.

Noruzy, A., Dalfard, V. M., Azhdari, B., Nazari-Shirkouhi, S., & Rezazadeh, A. (2013). Relations between transformational leadership, organizational learning, knowledge management, organizational innovation, and organizational performance: An empirical investigation of manufacturing firms. *The International Journal of Advanced Manufacturing Technology*, **64**, 1073–1085.

O'Connor, G. C. (1998). Market learning and radical innovation: A cross case comparison of eight radical innovation projects. *Journal of Product Innovation Management*, **15**, 151–166.

Oldham, G. R., & Cummings, A. (1996). Employee creativity: Personal and contextual factors at work. *Academy of Management Journal*, **39**, 607–634.

Osborn, R. N., & Marion, R. (2009). Contextual leadership, transformational leadership and the performance of international innovation seeking alliances. *The Leadership Quarterly*, **20**, 191–206.

Osburn, H. K., & Mumford, M. D. (2006). Creativity and planning: Training interventions to develop creative problem-solving skills. *Creativity Research Journal*, **18**, **173–190**.

Parnes, S. J., & Noller, R. B. (1972). Applied creativity: The creative studies project: Part results of a two-year study. *Journal of Creative Behavior*, **6**, **164–186**.

Patalano, A. L., & Seifert, C. M. (1997). Opportunistic planning: Being reminded of pending goals. *Cognitive Psychology*, **34**, **1–36**.

Paulus, P. B. (1989). *Psychology of group influence*. Hillsdale, NJ: L. Erlbaum.

Paulus, P. B., Dzindolet, M., & Kohn, N. W. (2012). Collaborative creativity—Group creativity and team innovation. In M. D. Mumford (Ed.), *Handbook of organizational creativity* (pp. **327–357**). Waltham, MA: Elsevier.

Paulus, P. B., & Yang, H. C. (2000). Idea generation in groups: A basis for creativity in organizations. *Organizational Behavior and Human Decision Processes*, **82**, **76–87**.

Perry, N. (1993). Scientific communication, innovation networks and organization structures. *Journal of Management Studies*, **30**, **957–973**.

Perry-Smith, J., & Shalley, C. E. (2003). The social side of creativity: A static and dynamic social network perspective. *Academy of Management Review*, **28**, **89–106**.

Peterson, N. G., Mumford, M. D., Borman, W. C., Jeanneret, P., & Fleishman, E. A. (1999). *An occupational information system for the 21st century: The development of O\* NET*. Washington, D.C.: American Psychological Association.

Putman, V. L., & Paulus, P. B. (2009). Brainstorming, brainstorming rules and decision making. *Journal of Creative Behavior*, **43**, **29–40**.

Qu, R., Janssen, O., & Shi, K. (2015). The effect of leader-member exchange and creativity expectations in predicting employee creativity. *Academy of Management Proceedings*, **2015, 15996**.

Ramey, C. H., & Weisberg, R. W. (2004). The "poetical activity" of Emily Dickinson: A further test of the hypothesis that affective disorders foster creativity. *Creativity Research Journal*, **16**, **173–185**.

Redmond, M. R., Mumford, M. D., & Teach, R. J. (1993). Putting creativity to work: Effects of leader behavior on subordinate creativity. *Organizational Behavior and Human Decision Processes*, **55**, **120–151**.

Rego, A., Sousa, F., Marques, C., & e Cunha, M. P. (2014). Hope and positive affect mediating the authentic leadership and creativity relationship. *Journal of Business Research*, **67**, **200–210**.

Reiter-Palmon, R. (2018). Creative cognition at the individual and team levels: What happens before and after idea generation. In R. Sternberg & J. Kaufman

(Eds.), *The nature of human creativity* (pp. **184**–**208**). New York: Cambridge University Press.

Reiter-Palmon, R., Mitchell, K. S., & Royston, R. (2019). Improving creativity in organizational settings. In J. C. Kaufman & R. J. Sternberg (Eds.), *The Cambridge handbook of creativity* (pp. **515**–**545**). Cambridge, UK: Cambridge University Press.

Reiter-Palmon, R., & Paulus, P. B. (2019). Cognitive and social processes in team creativity. In M. D. Mumford & E. M. Todd (Eds.), *Creativity and innovation in organizations* (pp. **161**–**190**). London: Routledge.

Rietzschel, E. F., Nijstad, B. A., & Stroebe, W. (2014). Effects of problem scope and creativity instructions on idea generation and selection. *Creativity Research Journal*, **26**, **185**–**191**.

Robledo, I. C., Peterson, D. R., & Mumford, M. D. (2012). Leadership of scientists and engineers: A three-vector model. *Journal of Organizational Behavior*, **33**, **140**–**147**.

Root-Bernstein, R. S., Bernstein, M., & Garnier, H. (1995). Correlations between avocations, scientific style, work habits, and professional impact of scientists. *Creativity Research Journal*, **8**, **115**–**137**.

Scherer, F. M. (1965). Firm size, market structure, opportunity, and the output of patented inventions. *The American Economic Review*, **55**, **1097**–**1125**.

Schippers, M. C., West, M. A., & Dawson, J. F. (2015). Team reflexivity and innovation: The moderating role of team context. *Journal of Management*, **41**, **769**–**788**.

Schoorman, F. D., Mayer, R. C., & Davis, J. H. (2007). An integrative model of organizational trust: Past, present, and future. *Academy of Management Review*, **32**, **344**–**354**.

Schult, A., & Wolff, M. (2012). *Strategic alignment of it and functional responsibilities in top management teams: An empirical performance study.* Washington, DC: Association for Information Systems.

Schumpeter, A. J. (2000). Entrepreneurship as innovation. In R. Swedberg (Ed.), *Entrepreneurship: A social science view* (pp. **51**–**75**). New Delhi: Oxford University Press.

Scott, G. M., Lonergan, D. C., & Mumford, M. D. (2005). Conceptual combination: Alternative knowledge structures, alternative heuristics. *Creativity Research Journal*, **17**, **21**–**36**.

Senge, P. M. (1995). *Learning organizations*. Cambridge: Gilmour Drummond.

Sethi, R., Smith, D. C., & Park, C. W. (2001). Cross-functional product development teams, creativity, and the innovativeness of new consumer products. *Journal of Marketing Research*, **38**, **73**–**85**.

Sheldon, K. M. (1995). Creativity and self-determination in personality. *Creativity Research Journal*, **8**, **25–36**.

Shin, S. J., Yuan, F., & Zhou, J. (2017). When perceived innovation job requirement increases employee innovative behavior: A sensemaking perspective. *Journal of Organizational Behavior*, **38**, 68–86.

Shin, S. J., & Zhou, J. (2003). Transformational leadership, conservation, and creativity: Evidence from Korea. *Academy of Management Journal*, **46**, **703–714**.

Shipman, A. S., Byrne, C. L., & Mumford, M. D. (2010). Leader vision formation and forecasting: The effects of forecasting extent, resources, and timeframe. *The Leadership Quarterly*, **21**, **439–456**.

Silverberg, G., & Verspagen, B. (1994). Learning, innovation and economic growth: A long-run model of industrial dynamics. *Industrial and Corporate Change*, **3**, **199–223**.

Simonton, D. K. (1984). *Genius, creativity, and leadership*. Cambridge, MA: Harvard University Press.

Smither, J. W. (2012). Performance management. In S. W. J. Kozlowski (Ed.), *The Oxford handbook of organizational psychology, Vol. 1* (pp. **285–329**). Oxford, UK: Oxford University Press.

Song, M., Dyer, B., & Thieme, R. J. (2006). Conflict management and innovation performance: An integrated contingency perspective. *Journal of the Academy of Marketing Science*, **34**, **341–356**.

Song, M., & Thieme, R. J. (2006). A cross-national investigation of the R&D–marketing interface in the product innovation process. *Industrial Marketing Management*, **35**, **308–322**.

Sosik, J. J., Kahai, S. S., & Avolio, B. J. (1998). Transformational leadership and dimensions of creativity: Motivating idea generation in computer-mediated groups. *Creativity Research Journal*, **11**, **111–121**.

Spreitzer, G. M., & Sonenshein, S. (2004). Toward the construct definition of positive deviance. *American Behavioral Scientist*, **47**, **828–847**.

Standish, C. J., Gujar, Y., & Mumford, M. D. (under review). Wisdom and leadership: Predicting leader performance with a new measure of wisdom. *The Leadership Quarterly*.

Sternberg, R. J. (1988). A three-facet model of creativity. In R. J. Sternberg (Ed.), *The nature of creativity* (pp. **125–148**). Cambridge: Cambridge University Press.

Strange, J. M., & Mumford, M. D. (2005). The origins of vision: Effects of reflection, models, and analysis. *The Leadership Quarterly*, **16**, **121–148**.

Sturdy, A., Clark, T., Fincham, R., & Handley, K. (2009). Between innovation and legitimation – boundaries and knowledge flow in management consultancy. *Organization*, **16**, **627–653**.

Styhre, A., & Gluch, P. (2009). Creativity and its discontents: Professional ideology and creativity in architect work. *Creativity and Innovation Management*, **18**, **224–233**.

Thamhain, H. J. (2011). Critical success factors for managing technology-intensive teams in the global enterprise. *Engineering Management Journal*, **23**, **30–36**.

Thamhain, H. J., & Gemmill, G. R. (1974). Influence styles of project managers: Some project performance correlates. *Academy of Management Journal*, **17**, **216–224**.

Tierney, P., & Farmer, S. M. (2002). Creative self-efficacy: Its potential antecedents and relationships to creative performance. *Academy of Management Journal*, **45**, **1137–1148**.

Tierney, P., Farmer, S. M., & Graen, G. B. (1999). An examination of leadership and employee creativity: The relevance of traits and relationships. *Personnel Psychology*, **52**, **591–620**.

Tjosvold, D., Tang, M. M., & West, M. (2004). Reflexivity for team innovation in China: The contribution of goal interdependence. *Group & Organization Management*, **29**, **540–559**.

Troy, L. C., Hirunyawipada, T., & Paswan, A. K. (2008). Cross-functional integration and new product success: An empirical investigation of the findings. *Journal of Marketing*, **72**, **132–146**.

Valle, S., & Avella, L. (2003). Cross-functionality and leadership of the new product development teams. *European Journal of Innovation Management*, **6**, **32–47**.

Van der Zee, K. I., Paulus, P., Vos, M., & Parthasarathy, N. (2009). The impact of group composition and attitudes towards diversity on anticipated outcomes of diversity in groups. *Group Processes & Intergroup Relations*, **12(2)**, **257–280**.

Van Knippenberg, D., & Schippers, M. C. (2007). Work group diversity. *Annual Review of Psychology*, **58**, **515–541**.

Vera, D., & Crossan, M. (2004). Strategic leadership and organizational learning. *Academy of Management Review*, **29**, **222–240**.

Vessey, W. B., Barrett, J. D., Mumford, M. D., Johnson, G., & Litwiller, B. (2014). Leadership of highly creative people in highly creative fields: A historiometric study of scientific leaders. *The Leadership Quarterly*, **25**, **672–691**.

Wallas, G. (1926). *The art of thought*. New York: Harcourt Brace Jovanovich.

Wang, A. C., & Cheng, B. S. (2010). When does benevolent leadership lead to creativity? The moderating role of creative role identity and job autonomy. *Journal of Organizational Behavior*, **31**, **106–121**.

Watts, L. L., Steele, L. M., & Song, H. (2017). Re-examining the relationship between need for cognition and creativity: Predicting creative problem-solving across multiple domains. *Creativity Research Journal*, **29**, **21–28**.

Wilson, J. M. (2014). Henry Ford vs. assembly line balancing. *International Journal of Production Research*, **52**, **757–765**.

Wise, G. (1992). Inventions and corporations in the maturing electrical industry. In R. J. Weber & D. N. Perkins (Eds.), *Inventive minds: Creativity in technology* (pp. **291–310**). New York: Oxford University Press.

Wong, P. K., Ho, Y. P., & Autio, E. (2005). Entrepreneurship, innovation and economic growth: Evidence from GEM data. *Small Business Economics*, **24**, **335–350**.

Yoshida, D. T., Sendjaya, S., Hirst, G., & Cooper, B. (2014). Does servant leadership foster creativity and innovation? A multi-level mediation study of identification and prototypicality. *Journal of Business Research*, **67**, **1395–1404**.

Yukl, G. (1998). *Leadership in organizations (4ᵗʰ ed.)*. Englewood Cliffs, NJ: Prentice Hall.

Yukl, G. (2011). Contingency theories of effective leadership. In A. Bryman, D. Collinson, K. Grint, B. Jackson, & M. Uhl-Bien (Eds.), *The Sage handbook of leadership* (pp. **286–298**). London: Sage.

Zaccaro, S. J., Connelly, S., Repchick, K. M. et al. (2015). The influence of higher order cognitive capacities on leader organizational continuance and retention: The mediating role of developmental experiences. *The Leadership Quarterly*, **26**, **342–358**.

Zhao, H., & Guo, L. (2019). The trickle-down effects of creative work involvement: The joint moderating effects of proactive personality and leader creativity expectations. *Personality and Individual Differences*, **142**, **218–225**.

Zhou, Q., Hirst, G., & Shipton, H. (2012). Promoting creativity at work: The role of problem-solving demand. *Applied Psychology: An International Review*, **61**, **56–80**.

Zuckerman, M. (1979). Attribution of success and failure revisited, or: The motivational bias is alive and well in attribution theory. *Journal of Personality*, **47**, **245–287**.

# Acknowledgments

We would like to thank Brandon Vessey, Gina Marie Ligon, Jill Strange, Blaine Gaddis, Jamie Barrett, Sam Hunter, Roni Reiter-Palmon, Sven Hemlin, Leif Denti, Per-Olof Larsson, and Shane Connelly for their contributions to the present effort. Correspondence should be addressed to Dr. Michael D. Mumford, Department of Psychology, University of Oklahoma, Norman, Oklahoma, 73019, or mmumford@ou.edu.

*To Quin and Kennis – The creative leaders of tomorrow.*

# Editor Biography

Dr. Michael D. Mumford is the George Lynn Cross Distinguished Research Professor of Psychology at The University of Oklahoma where he directs the Center for Applied Social Research. Dr. Mumford received his doctoral degree from the University of Georgia in 1983 in the fields of industrial and organizational psychology and psychometrics. He has more than 400 peer-reviewed publications in the areas of leadership, creativity, planning, and ethics. Dr. Mumford has served as senior editor of the *Leadership Quarterly* and the *Creativity Research Journal*. He sits on the editorial boards of the *Journal of Creative Behavior*, the *Psychology of Aesthetics, Creativity, and the Arts*, the *International Journal of Creativity and Problem-Solving*, the *Journal of Character and Leadership Development*, and *Group and Organization Management*, among other journals. Dr. Mumford is a fellow of the American Psychological Association (Divisions, 3, 5, 10, 14), the American Psychological Society, and the Society for Industrial and Organizational Psychology, and has served as president of the Society for Aesthetics, Creativity, and the Arts (Division 10). He has received more than $30 million in funding from the National Science Foundation, The National Institutes of Health, The National Aeronautics and Space Administration, The Department of Labor, The Department of State, The Department of Defense, and the Council of Graduate Schools. Dr. Mumford is a recipient of the Society for Industrial and Organizational Psychology's M. Scott Myers Award for applied research in the workplace, the Academy of Management's Eminent Leadership Scholar Award, and the American Psychological Association's Arnheim Award for career contributions to the study of creativity.

# Co-Author Biographies

Samantha England is a doctoral student in the University of Oklahoma's doctoral program in Industrial and Organizational Psychology. Her research interests include leadership, creativity, and innovation.

Mark W. Fichtel is a doctoral student in the University of Oklahoma's doctoral program in Industrial and Organizational Psychology. His research interests include creativity, leadership, and ethics.

Tanner R. Newbold is a doctoral student in the University of Oklahoma's doctoral program in Industrial and Organizational Psychology. His research interests include leadership, creativity, and innovation.

# Cambridge Elements ☰

# Leadership

## Ronald Riggio
*Claremont McKenna College*

Ronald E. Riggio, Ph.D. is the Henry R. Kravis Professor of Leadership and Organisational Psychology and former Director of the Kravis Leadership Institute at Claremont McKenna College. Dr. Riggio is a psychologist and leadership scholar with over a dozen authored or edited books and more than 150 articles/book chapters. He has worked as a consultant, and serves on multiple editorial boards.

## Susan Murphy
*University of Edinburgh*

Susan E. Murphy is Chair in Leadership Development at the University of Edinburgh Business School. She has published numerous articles and book chapters on leadership, leadership development, and mentoring. Susan was formerly Director of the School of Strategic Leadership Studies at James Madison University and Professor of Leadership Studies. Prior to that, she served as faculty and associate director of the Henry R. Kravis Leadership Institute at Claremont McKenna College. She also serves on the editorial board of The Leadership Quarterly.

## Georgia Sorenson
*University of Cambridge*

The late Georgia Sorenson, Ph.D. was the James MacGregor Burns Leadership Scholar at the Moller Institute and Moller By-Fellow of Churchill College at Cambridge University. Before coming to Cambridge, she founded the James MacGregor Burns Academy of Leadership at the University of Maryland, where she was Distinguished Research Professor. An architect of the leadership studies field, Dr. Sorenson has authored numerous books and refereed journal articles.

## About the Series

Cambridge Elements in Leadership is multi- and inter-disciplinary, and will have broad appeal for leadership courses in Schools of Business, Education, Engineering, Public Policy, and in the Social Sciences and Humanities.

# Cambridge Elements ⲉ

# Leadership

## Elements in the Series

Printed in the United States
by Baker & Taylor Publisher Services